AF240887

Student Prostitution Online

Distinction, Ambition and Ruptures

Eva Clouet

Student Prostitution Online

Distinction, Ambition and Ruptures

Max Milo Éditions
Collection Essais-Documents, Paris, 2023
www.maxmilo.com
ISBN : 978-2-31501-233-6

Acknowledgements

First of all, I'd like to thank my thesis supervisor, Karine Meslin, for her invaluable advice, encouragement and availability. I would also like to thank Anne-Marie Ledebt and the whole team at the Nantes delegation of Le Nid for their support and warm welcome throughout the year. Many thanks to Erwan for his patience... Thanks also to Dorian for his bright ideas, to Carole for her invaluable help, and to my family and friends who have supported and encouraged me in this work. Finally, I'd like to express my gratitude to all those who agreed to become my field of investigation, interviewees and respondents.

Foreword

Reflecting on prostitution is a fascinating exercise. When I chose to work on student prostitution for my Master 1 thesis, my ambition was not to make my results public. I wanted to take advantage of the time allotted to the preparation of a research project - the dissertation - to reflect on and try to gain a better understanding of a practice that raised questions for me, and which continues to do so. This writing is therefore part of an academic project. As a result, the results of this sociological investigation are not exhaustive, and many other aspects have not been addressed.

This study does not claim to be "the" truth about "student" prostitution - this subject remains wide open to research. On the contrary, this study is "a" truth about "a" student prostitution. The stories described correspond to the reality of some student prostitutes, including those of my interviewees.

Thanks to this work, I've learned a lot. And as I continue my research, I'm sure I'll learn many more things... But above all, this investigation has enabled me to meet some surprising, touching and thoughtful people. I'd like to thank them all once again for agreeing to meet me and for "laying themselves bare".

Without them, this study wouldn't exist... so thank you all again!
And keep your self-esteem intact...

Eva Clouet
November 2007

INTRODUCTION

Sexual issues are more topical than ever. Whether we're talking about inequalities between men and women, discrimination against sexual minorities, policies on parenthood and reproduction, pornography or prostitution, sexual and gendered issues - in other words, questions of gender and sexuality - intersect today to emerge as social and political issues. These issues concern individuals as much as the state, and the public space as much as the private sphere.

Last autumn, in the run-up to an election campaign, the issue of student prostitution appeared on the public agenda. The media linked the practice of student prostitution to the problems of economic insecurity affecting part of the student population. On October 30, 2006, *Le Figaro* ran the headline: "La prostitution gagne les bancs de la fac[1]" ("Prostitution wins over college benches"). According to the article, more and more female students in France are "selling their charms" to pay the rent or earn pocket money. The reason: the undeniable impoverishment of students. This article - like other sources on

---

1. PHILIBERT (Jean-Marc), "La prostitution gagne les bancs de la fac", *Le Figaro*, October 30, 2006, p. 11.

the subject - talks about student prostitutes, implying that this phenomenon only concerns girls.

Back in August, I came across this information in a leaflet from the SUD-Étudiant union, which estimated that "40,000 students were prostitutes in France". At the time, this revelation caught my attention, as I couldn't imagine - given the degraded and stigmatized image of prostitutes in the collective imagination - that prostitution could be "a student affair". Sensitive to this issue - in 2005-2006, I carried out a research project on the prostitution of immigrant women in the West - I began to investigate the question in order to shed some light on the "nature" of this prostitution and to understand what might be the reasons for this practice within the student world. This became the central theme of my Master 1 thesis.

As with all research work, I then had to translate "this general concern into a more limited theme and find an inter-knowledge group to start the field survey[2]."

After several weeks of investigation, it was finally on the Internet - via a discussion forum - that I came into contact with student prostitutes or, more accurately, "student escorts". I quickly realized that the prostitution practices of student escorts differed from those I had already worked on last year. Similarly, their motivations are not limited to the need for money, contrary to what the media would have us believe.

---

2. BEAUD (Stéphane) and WEBER (Florence), *Guide de l'enquête de terrain - Produire et analyser des données ethnographiques*, Éditions La Découverte, Paris, 1998, p. 28.

I have therefore focused my research on prostitution using new information and communication technologies. With this in mind, we'll be looking to see whether students who prostitute themselves via the Internet are prostitutes in a league of their own.

In the first part, we'll see that the theme of prostitution is at the heart of many issues that make its analysis complex, and that a wide variety of realities come together under the generic terms "prostitution" and "prostitute". Although male prostitution does exist (in France, around 10% of prostitutes are men), we will use the term "prostitute" to refer to both sexes, the spelling commonly used in the various references consulted. We will then look at the survey field and the conditions under which the material was collected.

In the second part, we'll highlight what distinguishes student escorts from other prostitutes, particularly in the way they conceive and envisage their practice.

Finally, in the last section, we'll try to better understand what leads some students to choose prostitution, by highlighting different forms of rupture that run through their life stories.

PART 1: SURVEY FRAMEWORK

1.1 PRESENTATION OF THE TOPIC

We all have an opinion on prostitution. It's an issue that is regularly debated, in the media and on the political stage[1]. However, the mechanisms behind it remain poorly understood. In this section, we'd like to show the limits of this spontaneous

---

1. Some recent examples of prostitution-related debates:

- On the eve of the soccer World Cup to be held in Germany from June 9 to July 9, 2006, a press conference was held at the Senate to denounce "the importation of 10,000 foreign women forced into prostitution in the *eros centers* (brothels in Germany) built for the occasion, near the soccer stadiums". The conference brought together political figures from all sides and activists from various groups fighting human trafficking;

- As early as spring 2006 and during the presidential campaign, several political parties - including the Socialist Party - opened the debate on the issue of penalizing customers (see in particular the article by Jacqueline Coignard, "Prostitution: le PS veut pénaliser les clients", *Libération*, July 6, 2006);

- July 13, 2007, 1 p.m. news on France 2: "The prostitutes' vans in Perrache will no longer be part of the scenery. Indeed, the Prefect of Lyon, Mr. Jacques Guéraut, says he is 'determined to see the government's directives applied at last."

knowledge, and we'll also try to unravel the threads that make up prostitution.

1.1.1 A complex theme imbued with strong ideologies

The idea that prostitution is first and foremost an individual act, even before being a social phenomenon[2] remains deeply rooted in common sense. However, as sociologist Saïd Bouamama points out, "prostitution should be seen as a social relationship, or more precisely as a complex of social relationships"[3]. Indeed, it is this articulation of several social relationships that makes debates and reflections on prostitution difficult, and sometimes confusing.

In our view, it is possible to identify two major elements underlying prostitution. These are the sexual relationship and the commercial relationship. Both relationships are marked by a process of domination: male domination and socio-economic domination[4].

Unequal gender relations at the root of the prostitution system

As far as male domination is concerned, it has to be said that even today, in all spheres of power (political, economic, access to education, etc.), women's place is downgraded and their

---

2. NOR (Malika), *La Prostitution*, Éditions Le Cavalier Bleu, Paris, 2001, p. 9.

3. BOUAMAMA (Saïd), *L'homme en question - Le processus du devenir-client de la prostitution*, Paris, 2004, p. 10.

4. Please refer to the "Conceptual model of the prostitution system applied to student prostitutes" (Appendix 1).

status is inferior to that of their male counterparts[5]. This reality, founded on a belief in women's inferiority, shapes the way society is organized.

Consequently, like other institutions, the prostitutional organization is at the heart of the patriarchal system. This is what feminist movements of all stripes, now supported by numerous scientists[6], are analyzing. Most of them adopt a critical and denunciatory stance.

As part of this movement, Claudie Lesselier[7] describes the prostitution system as "a particularly revealing manifestation of male domination". She explains that the way society functions and is organized is based on a system of unequal gender relations - thanks to which the prostitution system was instituted - which has, for several centuries now, conveyed "a set of stereotypes, beliefs, discriminations and sexist oppressions against women [as well as] a sexuality socially shaped in an

---

5. A few examples from France:

- In politics, despite the parity law passed in 2000, women are still in the minority in all political institutions (the Senate is undoubtedly the most striking example: only 17% women in 2004);

- At school, while girls are more numerous in seconde générale (55%), they are only 45% in première S, 25% in maths-physics preparatory classes and 15% at Polytechnique - MARRY (Catherine), *Les femmes ingénieures - une révolution respectueuse*, Belin, 2004 ;

- In terms of employment, 80% of the 3 million French people currently working for less than the minimum monthly wage are women - MARUANI (Margaret), *Femmes, genre et sociétés - L'état des savoirs*, La Découverte, 2005.

6. In the social sciences, sociologist Richard Poulin is a case in point.

7. Feminist founder of the French-based association RAJFIRE (Réseau pour l'autonomie juridique des femmes immigrées et réfugiées). Sources: FASTI website (Fédération des associations de solidarité avec les travailleurs immigrés), http://www.fasti.org/article.php3 ?id_article=403 [15/05/2007] - Dossier: *"Prostitution: l'exploitation des femmes étrangères"* - Compte rendu du forum national du 2 avril 2005.

unequal relationship between the sexes". According to her, "the existence of this system is born of the belief that women must be at the service of men and can be treated by them as objects." This echoes the analysis offered by anthropologist Paola Tabet when describing female sexuality. Her study shows that "girls' sexuality has to adapt to male demand[8]", and therefore female sexual activity takes on the appearance of "service" (she uses the expression "sexual service") to men, this being considered "natural".

Particularly since the 1970s, the state - influenced by feminist movements in particular - has been trying to mitigate this inequality by setting up a legal system[9], but changing mentalities doesn't happen overnight. "If in the past the question of women's submission was not raised, it has gradually emerged in the consciousness of women [and men] to the point of wanting to break the chains of this enslavement. But the more women tend towards this liberation, the more the fantasy of the submissive woman is present[10]." Even today, women's bodies and sexuality remain under the control of male judgment, a control they have

---

8. TABET (Paola), "La grande arnaque : l'expropriation de la sexualité des femmes", in Actuel Marx : *Les rapports sociaux de sexe*, n° 30, 2001, p. 146

9. Some examples of legislation (in France):

- In 1972, the principle of equal pay was enshrined in the French Labour Code;

- In 1981, a Ministry of Women's Rights was created and entrusted to Yvette Roudy;

- In 1983, the Roudy law promoted professional equality between men and women;

- In 1999, the Constitution was revised: "the law favors equal access of women and men to electoral mandates and elective functions". AUTAIN (Clémentine), *Les Droits des femmes - l'inégalité en question*, Éditions Milan, 2003.

10. SCHAFF (Christelle), *Prostitution en France : l'enquête*, Éditions de la Lagune, 2007, p. 26-27.

largely internalized[11]. The prostitution system is based on this division of the sexes.

At the heart of the prostitution system, a relationship and domination based on money

In prostitution, domination is also exercised through money. For a long time, money was legally a male domain - women were considered eternally minors. In France, until 1938, a woman was not allowed to open a bank account without her husband's authorization. Moreover, it was only in 1965 that she was granted the freedom to exercise a profession without her husband's consent... but there's still some way to go before she can dispose of her salary autonomously!

Today, although the majority of women in our society work and no longer depend on resources other than their own, economic difficulties continue to hit them harder than men. These various inequalities - lower wages, more frequent unemployment, less remunerative jobs, etc. - can be explained by the sexual division of labor which, according to Christine Delphy's analysis, "is embodied in the patriarchal and economic system in place[12]". As we know, entry into prostitution is often linked to a need for money due to a more or less difficult economic situation. What's more, in the prostitutional relationship, "money calls for the same role-playing as that instituted by the patriarchal system: the buyer is the one who dominates[13]". This shows just how much power and domination are at stake in paid sex,

---

11. BOURDIEU (Pierre), *La Domination masculine*, Éditions du Seuil, Paris, 1998.

12. DELPHY (Christine), *L'Ennemi principal (tome I)*, Éditions Syllepses, Paris, 1998, p. 118.

13. SCHAFF (Christelle), *op. cit.* p. 27.

which once again works to the disadvantage of women. We can see here that the effects of socio-economic domination mirror those of male domination.

A controversial subject

The complexity of the subject of prostitution and the issues involved make it controversial and difficult to objectify. As a result, prostitution is a subject that mobilizes passions and affects.

Prostitution, as a social fact, has been the subject of passionate debate for many years[14]. From its very inception[15], "politicians, religious reformers, medical authorities, the scientific community and feminist groups have debated whether the sex trade should be legalized, banned, tolerated or abolished[16]." This debate is still going on today, and still pits various players on the social and political scene against each other.

The way in which the prostitution phenomenon is viewed (and consequently the analyses produced on the subject) are imbued with strong ideologies that very often "detract from the objectivity of the findings[17]". In this respect, all the references consulted for this study support, more or less explicitly, a particular vision of prostitution. Malika Nor reminds us in her book that these ideological positions are "unavoidable [because] the suffering and contempt engendered by this phenomenon

---

14. BOUAMAMA (Saïd), *op. cit.* p. 9.

15. Prostitution, in its modern, venal form, appeared in Greece in the 4th century B.C. through the *dicterions*, "state houses" and ancestors of the "brothels".

16. PETHERSON (Gail), *op. cit.* p. 180.

17. NOR (Malika), *op. cit.* p. 117

demand that we take a stand[18]." Against this backdrop, it's no easy task to approach this issue with impartiality. Let's take a closer look at what these different ideologies cover.

Two distinct visions of prostitution divide public, political and media opinion. On the one hand, as Sylvie Bigot points out, prostitution can be approached from the angle of human trafficking and violence against women. Using the figure of the foreign prostitute exploited by a pimp, the subject of prostitution "causes a sensation at its most horrifying[19]". According to Christelle Schaff, this discourse, put forward by various[20] collectives and relayed by a number of media, serves to "sensitize opinion and public authorities to the most shocking and unacceptable aspects of prostitution[21]". On the other hand, for some years now, prostitutes have been invited on media platforms to loudly proclaim their "freedom of choice". There are no half-measures when it comes to prostitution: women are either victimized and exploited, or presented as fulfilled, extroverted and free.

This duality illustrates the fact that the subject of prostitution is a hotly contested ideological issue. Supporters of these ideologies generally clash over two essential points: the existence

---

18. NOR (Malika), *ibid.*

19. BIGOT (Sylvie), L'épanouissement sexuel des femmes au travers de l'escorting : mythe ou réalité ? *Journée regards insolites sur la sexualité - Regards artistiques et sociologiques sur la sexualité*, Paris, École normale supérieure, June 2, 2007.

20. This mainly concerns abolitionist associations, some of which are: "Aux Captifs, La Libération"; "Équipes d'Action Contre le Proxénétisme - EACP"; "Fondation Scelles".

21. SCHAFF (Christelle), *op. cit.* p. 20.

or otherwise of voluntary prostitution, and the status to be accorded to prostitution. The former believe that prostitution is a form of exploitation that should be abolished. The others claim that it is an activity like any other, possibly chosen, which should be regulated. This is the main difference between abolitionists and regulationists.

A regulatory approach and regime

Historically, the authorities' first reaction to prostitution was to regulate it. Regulators saw prostitution as an unavoidable fact that needed to be organized in order to control it.

This ideology, born of the desire to "restore public and moral order[22]" and then taken up by hygienist theories, led the powers that be to organize prostitution. The public authorities assigned places where prostitution could be practiced in accordance with the law: districts - Amsterdam's famous "Red Light District" - brothels or "eros centers".

In France, the regulatory regime was in operation for part of the Middle Ages. The Church, which was "more comfortable with the trade in women than with destructive sexual freedom[23]", developed a pragmatic approach to prostitutes. As early as the end of Antiquity, Saint Augustine declared: "They are to the city what a cloaca is to the palace. Remove the cloaca, and the palace becomes a vile place. Remove the prostitutes, and the passions will turn the world upside down; give them the rank of honest women, and dishonor will blight the universe[24]." From

---

22. SCHAFF (Christelle), *ibid.* p. 85.
23. NOR (Malika), *ibid.* p. 17.
24. NOR (Malika), *ibid.*

then on, prostitutes were despised, but forgiven, as they were considered "the impurity necessary to preserve the integrity of other women[25]". From the 11th century onwards, and more intensely from the 14th century onwards, those responsible for public order - secular or ecclesiastical lords - considered prostitution to be "a lesser evil", and so organized and supervised the activity, while at the same time making substantial profits from it. Towns and cities thus officially opened "municipal houses of prostitution", or designated neighborhoods - usually suburbs - where prostitution would be permitted. Although "tolerated", prostitutes remained excluded and stigmatized - for example, they were obliged to wear a different outfit from non-prostitute women, so that the latter would not be bothered. The ideal for these "lost women" is that "after having fulfilled their duties for a time, they repent and save their souls[26]", in the image of Mary Magdalene.

From the mid-sixteenth to the end of the eighteenth century, the tendency to organize prostitution was reversed, and the idea of closing houses became widespread throughout Europe[27]. Then, at the beginning of the nineteenth century, the regulatory regime was once again adopted. In the aftermath of the French Revolution, the institution of "maisons closes" (or "brothels") in France was prompted by the resurgence of venereal diseases, which prostitutes were suspected of causing. Henceforth, pros-

---

25. NOR (Malika), *ibid.*

26. Wikipedia, the free encyclopedia [07/23/2007], http://fr.wikipedia.org/wiki/Histoire_de_la_prostitution.

27. In France, the proscription ordinance dates back to 1560, but the measures pronounced remain little enforced. Moreover, this position did not curb the prostitution phenomenon, as it developed and organized itself underground.

titution was tolerated, and "it was appropriate for the public authorities to regulate it in order to better control it"[28]. In 1796, at the instigation of the Directoire, Napoleon ordered the establishment of a register of prostitution in Paris, and subjected "public women" to the police. In 1802, a decree established compulsory medical examinations for prostitutes, with the aim of stemming the syphilis epidemic. Then, as the State no longer wished to interfere directly in "matters of morality", it offloaded the responsibility to the administration and the "morality police", created for the occasion. In this context, "the organization and operation of brothels resembled the prison system[29]. The prostitutes who work in these establishments are listed under a number (they are called "numbered prostitutes"). Similarly, prostitutes working on the street (and therefore outside the brothels) are "carded", and the "insubordinate" (unlisted, and therefore clandestine) are hunted down by law enforcement officials.

Until the 1830s, the brothel also served as a place for the exchange of alcohol and food. Then, throughout the 19th century, its purpose as a "place for all kinds of pleasures[30]" became increasingly clear. From then on, "prostitutes became specialized workers, professional soothers, love drainers[31]" and "a visit to the brothel became the norm, not to say a social rite[32]". Brothels rapidly multiplied (in Paris alone, there were some two hundred official establishments by 1850), and their frequentation by a number of artists helped make them fashionable. Until

---

28. ADLER (Laure), *ibid.* p. 16.
29. NOR (Malika), *op. cit.* p. 22.
30. ADLER (Laure), *op. cit.* p. 18.
31. ADLER (Laure), *ibid.* p. 14.
32. NOR (Malika), *op. cit.* p. 23.

the beginning of the 20th century, writers and painters "became observers of their time [...] and offered a romantic vision of the brothel [...] where the prostitute embodied a troubled and fascinating figure[33]." On the other hand, the reality of women's living conditions in brothels is often overlooked.

Today, although France has abandoned the regulatory system, it is still in force in several European countries, including Germany, Greece and the Netherlands.

Opponents of this system - abolitionists in particular - denounce the trivialization of prostitution that its regulation entails.

Abolitionist conception and regime

The abolitionist ideology - born in reaction to the regulationist trend - aims to abolish the regulation of prostitution and, ultimately, envision a prostitution-free society. Proponents of this ideology argue that "in regulationist countries, the number of prostitutes is very high[34]". They also explain that most prostitutes prefer "clandestinity to administrative registration and official labelling". Finally, abolitionists denounce the fact that the institutionalization of prostitution facilitates the establishment of criminal networks, and serves as a cover for the establishment of parallel illegal practices, such as the arms and drugs trades.

This position emerged in Great Britain in the 1870s at the initiative of feminist Joséphine Butler, who considered that "the system of prostitution constitutes a contemporary form of

---

33. NOR (Malika), *ibid.* p. 22-23.

34. LEGARDINIER (Claudine), *Prostitution - 100 mots pour comprendre*, Mouvement du Nid, Clichy, 2005, p. 56.

slavery which oppresses women[35]". At the same time, in France, feminists such as Avril de Sainte-Croix relayed this ideology. They railed against the powers that be, who "in addition to denying women all civic freedom, are also depriving them of all sexual freedom[36]". The abolitionist movement denounced the living conditions of house prostitutes, whom it likened to "white slaves, human crumbs, toys of debauchery[37]". From the beginning of the 20th century, "a veritable propaganda campaign" - backed by socialists and libertarians, relayed by some of the press and supported by the likes of Jean Jaurès and Émile Zola - "tried to gain political acceptance for the theses of abolitionism[38]". However, this movement had only a relative impact on attitudes and policies. Although the vice police were abolished, hygienic theories were promoted and prostitution remained "a necessary evil[39]".

It wasn't until the end of the Second World War that French policy embraced the abolitionist point of view. On April 13 1946, the Marthe Richard law ordered the official closure of brothels on the grounds that "liberated France must ensure an honest and dignified existence for all[40]". In practice, however, this law did not put an end to prostitution, which continued to develop in other forms: studios, "hôtels de passe", roadsides, massage parlors...

---

35. SCHAFF (Christelle), *op. cit.* p. 86.

36. NOR (Malika), *ibid.* p. 22-23.

37. ADLER (Laure), *op. cit.* p. 240.

38. ADLER (Laure), *ibid.* p. 241.

39. The fight for a "clean" brothel then began: the Lépine law (in 1900) more or less chaotically kept "the meeting house" within a system of regulation and health surveillance.

40. NOR (Malika), *op. cit.* p. 24.

In 1960, France signed the UN Convention - drafted in 1949[41] - for the Suppression of the Traffic in Persons and of the Exploitation of the Prostitution of Others. This clearly marked the country's entry into an abolitionist regime for prostitution: the prostitute was considered a victim, pimping and any legislative framework for the legalization of prostitution were prohibited.

In view of the current situation, however, these various laws have only had a limited effect, as prostitution adapts and continues to make money. Similarly, in view of the different positions adopted by several European partners (in Germany, the Netherlands, Greece... prostitution is legal and regulated), the question of regulating prostitution is still being debated in France, and the possible reopening of brothels remains on the agenda.

The main critics of this ideology - regulatory feminists among them - denounce the "hypocrisy" and "limited effect" of abolitionist legislation. They take the example of France, which "despite its abolitionist regime, still has prostitution[42]". They also underline the "infantilizing character" in which abolitionists hold prostitutes: "considered as victims and therefore incapable of knowing what is good for them, prostitutes are maintained in a status of inferiority by a confiscation of the word for the benefit of those who are supposed to get them out of there[43]!" In

---

41. At international level, the abolitionist regime was established with the 1949 Convention, ratified more or less rapidly by several European countries, including the United Kingdom, Spain and France.

42. NOR (Malika), *op. cit.* p. 31.

43. NIKITA (Maîtresse) and SCHAFFAUSER (Thierry), *Fières d'être putes*, Éditions l'Altiplano, Paris, 2007, p. 24.

this sense, abolitionists are accused of denying prostitutes their "freedom of choice".

Another form of legislation: the prohibitionist regime

Alongside these first two positions, there's a third, albeit less prominent. This is the prohibitionist regime which, as its name suggests, prohibits and condemns the entire prostitution chain: pimps, prostitutes and customers.

This system prevailed in France from the 17th to the 19th century. At the time, the State was determined to combat prostitution, considered a "scourge" due to the spread of venereal diseases. The various measures aimed at eradicating prostitution were once again designed to guarantee moral order, but also to protect public health. However, these ordinances only concerned prostitutes, and gradually established "a system of confinement[44]" for those who indulged in this "perversion". Asylums" were soon opened for "repentant women", soon to be joined "by those considered at risk of falling into prostitution because they were poor, unmarried or too tempting because they were too pretty[45]." As England began deporting prostitutes from "closed houses" to the West Indies, Louis XIV ordered in 1658 that all women "guilty of prostitution, fornication or adultery be imprisoned at the Salpêtrière until the priests or nuns in charge consider that they have repented and changed[46]".

Today, this system still exists in the Gulf States, in part of China, and in a few states in the United States.

---

44. LEGARDINIER (Claudine), *La Prostitution*, éditions Milan, Paris, 1996, p. 7.

45. Wikipedia, the free encyclopedia [07/23/2007], http://fr.wikipedia.org/wiki/Histoire_de_la_prostitution.

46. Wikipedia, the free encyclopedia, *ibid.*

With regard to this legislation, regulators and abolitionists agree that this regime is "incapable of solving the problem of prostitution[47]" and that one of the harmful consequences of this prohibition lies in "the clandestine organization of prostitution[48]".

From the 1960s-1970s, the place of women and questions relating to sexuality ("autonomous sexuality", "sexual freedom", etc.) were put forward by a number of women and feminist groups. In this context, debates on prostitution have been given a new lease of life. It is therefore important for us to reconstruct the role of feminists in this history.

Prostitution and feminist views

Since the new feminist wave of the 1970s, which considered "the private as political" and placed sexuality at the heart of women's struggles, prostitution has become one of the working themes of women theorists and activists. For over thirty years now, "the ideological and strategic tension between those who recognize prostitution as work and those who define it as violence against women has become a point of fierce political split in international feminism[49]." Today, this debate continues and is far from over.

Abolitionist feminists - such as Catherine McKinnon in the USA and Marie-Victoire Louis or Malka Marcovitch in France -

---

47. LEGARDINIER (Claudine), *op. cit.*, p. 52.

48. NOR (Malika), *op. cit.* p. 29.

49. PETHERSON (Gail), "Prostitution I", in HIRATA (N.), LABORIE (F.), LE DAORE (H.) and SENOTIER (D.), *Dictionnaire critique du féminisme*, 2000, 2nd expanded edition, PUF, p. 182.

define sexuality as "a source of domination" and analyze it in its most violent dimensions, such as rape, prostitution, pornography and so on. With this in mind, they work to ensure that the State intervenes more rigorously to prohibit and condemn violence against women.

In contrast, regulatory or "pro-sex" feminists - such as Gayle Rubin and Judith Butler in the USA, and Marie-Hélène Bourcier and Beatriz Preciado in France - see sexuality as a "place of experimentation" that "cannot be reduced to gender domination". From this perspective, prostitution should be a matter of "free choice" and "women's self-determination". Prostitutes are considered "active" in the act of prostitution, which is why these feminists refer to them as "sex workers".

The "Les Putes" movement, born in October 2005 at the European Conference of Sex Workers, brings together prostitutes from various European countries. These men, women and transgendered people want to improve the conditions under which prostitution is practiced, and refuse to "continue to bear the stigma attached to prostitution[50]". They are even more strongly opposed to the abolitionist ideology than the regulationists. Although often assimilated to the regulationist current, this movement does not wish to see the opening of brothels as they currently exist and are organized in several European countries. For the proponents of this vision, "the regulation of sex work must be in the interests of working women, and not for the benefit of pimps converted into bosses[51]." Opposed to salaried

---

50. NIKITA (Maîtresse) and SCHAFFAUSER (Thierry), *op. cit.* p. 11.
51. NIKITA (Maîtresse) and SCHAFFAUSER (Thierry), *ibid.* p. 24.

employment, these women demand self-employed status, and envisage prostitution establishments run by themselves.

Since time immemorial, prostitution has been a source of heated controversy: human trafficking for some - who advocate abolitionism - and a necessary and freely chosen activity that should be regulated and organized for others. In the 1970s, France, alternately a regulator and an abolitionist, saw the emergence of new representations of prostitution.

The emergence of new representations of prostitution and prostitutes

1970s: the emergence of free prostitution

In 1970s France, the prostitute embodied the image of the "liberated woman", as opposed to the woman "trapped" in the structure of marriage. The prostitute "became the very emblem of the rebellious, rebellious woman, controlling her sexuality and opposing the moral order[52]. So it was in a political, social and cultural context in turmoil that free and voluntary prostitution emerged. It was against this backdrop that the first prostitutes' movement was launched in the spring of 1975. Several hundred prostitutes marched through the streets of Lyon, then occupied a church to "protest against the repressive policies of the time and against the new bill condemning them to heavy fines, thus increasing the risk of prison[53]." This event placed prostitution "at

---

52. SCHAFF (Christelle), *op. cit.* p. 87.
53. NIKITA (Maîtresse) and SCHAFFAUSER (Thierry), *op. cit.* p. 47.

the forefront of France's social problems[54], and the prostitutes' demands received the support of part of the press and public opinion. Despite these mobilizations and the growing awareness of "free prostitution", the Giscard government passed the law in the summer of 1975.

1980s: AIDS and international prostitution networks

In the 1980s, the issue of prostitution reappeared on the political scene: first from a public health perspective - in connection with the AIDS epidemic - and then in view of the recent extension of the international nature of prostitution - then described as "trafficking" in women. At the same time, the prostitutes' movement is still alive and well, and their fight against "police and social discrimination and for recognition of their full rights as citizens and workers[55]" remains a topical one. However, their demands are no longer supported either by public opinion or by major feminist groups, who accuse these prostitutes of "serving the interests of pimps[56]". As a result, some feminists are turning their attention from "these false victims" to "improving the lot of the real ones, [i.e.] women who are sexually harassed or exploited in their bodies[57]". As for the Socialist government in power, it maintains fiscal and police repression of prostitution, in exchange for new subsidies for social workers and victim support associations.

---

54. SOLE (Jacques), *L'Âge d'or de la prostitution - de 1879 à nos jours*, Plon, Paris, 1994, p. 139.

55. PETHERSON (Gail), *op. cit.* p. 182.

56. SOLE (Jacques), *op. cit.* p. 142.

57. SOLE (Jacques), *ibid.* p. 642.

1990-2000: "Sex industry" and displacement of prostitution

In the years 1990-2000, debates on prostitution resurfaced, again in connection with AIDS, but above all with the notion of "modern slavery" linked to the development and intensification of national and international prostitution networks. In France, the arrival of large numbers of foreign women forced into street prostitution prompted the government to take radical measures. Prostitution networks became the "workhorse" of politicians, who stepped up their criminalization in order to stem the flow of foreign populations. In practice, these measures are mainly reflected in "a policy of cleaning up urban centers[58]". It was against this backdrop that, in 2002, Nicolas Sarkozy, then Minister of the Interior, proposed his draft laws on internal security. These laws, which came into force in 2003, increased the penalties for pimping and re-established the notion of "passive soliciting".

For the past four years, the prostitution debate has focused on these laws, and in particular on their perverse effects. For once, feminists and collectives of all stripes agree: the internal security laws have in no way eliminated prostitution, but they have helped to make it less visible. Although prostitutes have partly fled the sidewalks, prostitution is still thriving. As Claudine Legardinier explains, it has "become more clandestine, more mobile and more discreet[59]". As a result, since the implementation of these measures, "the mutation of the places where prostitution is practiced has only accelerated[60]". So much so that today, there are as many prostitution venues as there are ways of prostituting oneself.

---

58. SCHAFF (Christelle), *op. cit.* p. 110.

59. LEGARDINIER (Claudine), *La Prostitution*, éditions Milan, Paris, 1996, p. 16.

60. SCHAFF (Christelle), *op. cit.* p. 120.

1.1.2 *"Prostitution"*

According to anthropologist and political scientist Janine Mossuz-Lavau, it's more appropriate today to talk about *prostitution* rather than *prostitution* "given the diversity of situations[61]". Each location (studios, bars, clubs, massage parlors, freeway service areas, woods, vans, etc.) has its own prostitution reality, with its own codes, its own specific features, its own rates, its own clientele, its own constraints and its own issues. At the same time, it would seem that these realities refer to two ways of prostituting oneself: on the one hand, there are women freed from pimps, who choose to engage in this activity; and on the other, women who are victims of human trafficking, forced and coerced to sell sexual services for the benefit of mafia-pimping networks of all kinds[62]. While this distinction between "free prostitution" and "forced prostitution" is not new - historians point out that as early as the 1920s, "the desire to prostitute was put forward, and [this activity] appeared for some women as a choice, even as a liberation[63]" - it seems more topical than ever, as Maîtresse Nikita and Thierry Schaffauser point out in their book: "We are whores, and proud of it[64]". The arrival of new means of communication (Minitel, Internet, cell phones) seems to have reinforced this divide.

---

61. MOSSUZ-LAVAU (Janine) and HANDMAN (Marie-Élisabeth), *La Prostitution à Paris*, Éditions de la Martinière, Paris, 2005, p. 13.

62. Janine Mossuz-Lavau refers to the former as "traditional" and the latter as "slaves"; MOSSUZ-LAVAU (Janine) and HANDMAN (Marie-Élisabeth), *ibid.*, p. 397.

63. ADLER (Laure), *op. cit.* p. 245.

64. NIKITA (Maîtresse) and SCHAFFAUSER (Thierry), *op. cit.*

New technologies and the development of individual, independent prostitution

With the Internet and advances in telecommunications, prostitution has changed. Pascal Lardellier's study of love encounters via specialized online sites confirms this observation. According to him, "the arrival of the Internet has facilitated the quest for virtual sex - 'cybersex' - or real sex, via dating networks or other explicit sites. The Web has become the biggest brothel ever, with its alcoves, boudoirs and millions of secret passageways to all kinds of online pleasures.[65]"

Minitel and pink messengers, ancestors of the Internet

Before the Internet, the Minitel of the 1980s was already paving the way for a particular form of prostitution. The famous "pink messaging services" were "an excellent solicitation tool, the benefits of which were immediately recognized by the prostitution industry[66]". In addition to the hosts employed to maintain "naughty" dialogues for a fee with lust-seekers[67] and the explicit advertisements of "pimped" prostitutes, a number of "independent" prostitutes (often ex-street prostitutes), as well as "anonymous" ones, use this medium to make contact with customers. In fact, the customers I met for my study both spoke of the experiences they'd had using Minitel (see Michel's interview extract in the box).

---

65. LARDELLIER (Pascal), *Le Cœur NET - Célibat et amour sur le Web*, Paris, Éditions Belin, 2004, p. 180.

66. CHALEIL (Max), *Prostitution - Le désir mystifié*, Éditions l'Aventurine, Paris, 2002, p. 242.

67. See Karin BERNFELD's novel *Alice au pays des femelles*, Éditions Balland, 2001, 314 p.

Internet, fast, easy and... discreet

The Minitel, and now the Internet, offer significant advantages, both for customers (demand) and for those wishing to prostitute themselves (supply). In addition to the wide choice and regular updates, the Internet makes it possible, at any time and in any place, to make discreet, low-cost encounters with complete peace of mind, as it offers "comfortable, secure anonymity[68]". What's more, the Internet obviously makes police action more laborious: "prostitutes operating on the Net don't risk much, because even if they can be worried about soliciting, they're not a priority for the police[69]."

Michel, customer of occasional prostitutes

I meet Michel in a café in central Paris. He introduces himself as a courteous, polite man, and seems to enjoy being interviewed. Michel has been married for some twenty years to a woman "[he] loves and admires" and holds a position of "responsibility". He began meeting prostitutes before he was married, when he was "young and shy". At the time, Michel "didn't have much money" and met exclusively street prostitutes. About ten years ago, he resumed venal encounters via Minitel, but this time Michel prefers to meet women who prostitute themselves "on a very, very occasional basis!" Today, Michel maintains "regular relationships" with a few occasional escorts - some of whom are also students - whom he contacts mainly via a Web discussion forum.

Michel: " [...] And then when I started up again about ten years ago, it was more via Minitel, which at the time worked

---

68. LARDELLIER (Pascal), *op. cit.*, p. 65.

69. Extract from the "notes d'intention" by author and director Yann Reuzeau for the play *Les débutantes - Prostituées en quelques clics*.

well... Well, now it's completely *outdated*, but there were sites on Minitel that specialized in the subject, where you knew that all the women were prostitutes and the men were clients. So the Minitel was the way to get in touch, and there too it was good, although I wouldn't say as good a guarantee of quality as the Forum, but there were still some very occasional women. And so they used the Minitel to meet people like that, but I don't think they would ever have dared to post an ad, and certainly not to go out on the street! So they were able to meet people in their own homes, discreetly! And without necessarily giving out their phone number straight away."

In this context, many ex-street prostitutes and others are starting up their own business. Of course, not all Net prostitutes are independent: many work on behalf of "agencies", and some are under pressure from pimps, notably with the introduction of "tours"[70], veritable slave networks[71]. But it's clear that the Internet is overturning many obstacles, making it easier for some women to choose prostitution. Sacha Love's story is a case in point. The woman, a hotel manager who was currently in financial difficulties, found "the miracle job that would save

---

70. *On-tour prostitute*: A prostitute/escort who works for a pimp. The pimp installs her for a period - more or less short - in a hotel in a major Western city, where she receives a large number of clients every day (often more than ten a day), and then moves her to another city. Recruitment networks (mostly in Eastern Europe) and solicitation are carried out via the Web. The term *on tour* indicates that the prostitute is "on tour", making the "rounds" of major Western cities.

71. In May 2000, a complementary office to the OCRETH (Office central de répression de la traite des êtres humains) was created to combat crime linked to new technologies. The OCLCTIC (Office central de lutte contre la criminalité liée aux technologies de l'information et de la communication) is responsible for dealing with minor offences as well as pimping-related crimes.

me from the wreckage" on the Web: "The next morning, I went online. It's easy enough to come across lists of escorts, dozens of specialized sites [...] The girls display themselves in lascivious poses, without revealing anything about their specialties. [...] I sign up, mechanically filling in boxes. Asked for a pseudonym, I choose Sacha. I continue with the registration. Age: thirty-two. Weight? I weigh two kilos to make myself look my best. City: Paris. Sport: Riding. Smoker: No. [...] The 'Sacha' page appeared on the 'France-Escort' website the following Saturday. I instantly received a flurry of calls and emails [...][72]."

New technologies and the emergence of escorting

Escort, Net prostitute

On the Net, the most visible offers of paid sex are those of "escorts". Originally, "escorting" consisted of escorting a person (usually a man), i.e. accompanying them to parties, restaurants, theaters, etc. In this context, sex is not part of the contract (and therefore not obligatory), but remains an implicit intention, considered a private act between the escort and her client. This ambiguity justifies the fact that the escort is often likened to a "luxury prostitute", as she responds to a specific demand. "Charm, beauty and distinction are demanded of her, but so are the intellectual qualities that enable her to accompany her clients, who are often socially well-off men[73]." Today, the "escort" business still exists (mainly through agencies). But the

---

72. LOVE (Sacha), *Escort girl, le récit d'une double vie*, Alban Éditions, Paris, 2006, p. 39-42.

73. SCHAFF (Christelle), *op. cit.* p. 50.

term "escort" is now used by all prostitutes operating on the Net, whatever the "level" of their service. As a result, the term "escort" hides a wide range of realities: "Former street prostitutes driven off the street, professionals with busy schedules, foreigners exploited by networks, or occasional 'night beauties'[74]."

The Internet as an escort showcase[75]

Escorts solicit and communicate through advertisements on specialized or general sites, which often include a section called "venal encounters" or "adult encounters". These ads mainly feature practical information about the services on offer. For example, we find the measurements of the escort, her age, the region or town in which she works, her availability, her rates, and sometimes a brief paragraph detailing her services, as well as her "taboos[76]".

A number of escorts also have their own website or blog[77]. These personalized sites, generally basic in their design and interface, often present themselves in the same way. First, a window opens, stating that the user must be of legal age to continue the investigation. Upon entering the site, a text - written by the escort herself - gives a more or less detailed presentation of herself. Some simply describe themselves physically, while

---

74. FRANCHON (Matthieu) and BITESNICH (Andreas), "Salariées le jour, escort girls la nuit", *Choc* (hebdomadaire), June 28 2007, n° 87, p. 26-33.

75. Expression borrowed from Sylvie BIGOT, *op. cit.*

76. In escorting jargon, "taboos" refer to sexual practices that the escort refuses to engage in as part of a venal relationship. In contrast, "taboo-free" refers to an escort who accepts all kinds of practices.

77. *Blog* : A website made up of a collection of posts arranged in chronological order. Each post (also called a note or article) is, like a diary or journal, an addition to the blog. The *blogger* (i.e., the person who keeps the blog) contributes a text, often enriched with hyperlinks and multimedia elements, which readers can generally comment on.

others talk about their interests, marital status, reasons for prostituting themselves... This text also enables the escort to set out her expectations of the encounter and the customer's behavior (meeting conditions, tastes in sexual practices, type of man...). Next, a number of headings specify the nature of the service offered by the escort. Generally speaking, we find a list of possible services and those that the escort refuses; rates (by the hour, evening, night or more); availability ("working hours"); and finally the contact page where the escort enters her e-mail and/or cell phone number. The "photo gallery" often illustrates the blog and shows the escort in different lights.

We can see that escorts who show their faces in their photographs are rare. In fact, this "precaution" only concerns a certain category of escorts. Generally speaking, those who choose to conceal their faces do so essentially to preserve their identity, because those around them are unaware of their prostitution and/or escorting is not their only activity. Often, these women have another "official" activity and prostitute themselves on an occasional basis.

New technologies and the democratization of "non-professional" and occasional prostitution

Despite the recent media hype, the phenomenon of occasional prostitution is not new. As far back as 1919, Abraham Flexner, in his definition of prostitution, highlighted the ephemeral and occasional nature of the practice[78]. Similarly, in

---

78. FLEXNER (Abraham), *La Prostitution en Europe*, 1919, in ADLER (Laure), *op. cit.*, p. 16.

her book written over ten years ago, Claudine Legardinier also refers to this occasional form of prostitution, explaining that it is essentially a question of "rounding off the ends of the month[79]". The Internet seems to have democratized this alternative.

Occasional prostitution, a double life

As its name suggests, occasional prostitution is a punctual and irregular practice. As such, it is the opposite of "professional" prostitution, which operates in the same way as most professions, i.e., a daily activity within a precise time frame. Occasional prostitution is more of an "extra", as it is carried out alongside another professional activity. In other words, for the professional prostitute, prostitution represents her main activity and source of income, whereas the occasional prostitute is a secretary, housewife, lawyer, job seeker, student... and prostitute in her spare time; prostitution remains a secondary activity. From this point of view, the occasional worker is generally independent (she works for herself, on her own account) and prostitution is a personal choice.

Malika Nor[80] points out that occasional independent prostitutes are generally unknown to social services. She adds that "this type of voluntary prostitution is generally motivated by money, either because this activity proves to be extremely luxurious and lucrative, or because for these people it only represents a source of income that is complementary or necessary to a minimum subsistence level." So, for the author, occasional and indepen-

---

79. LEGARDINIER (Claudine), *La Prostitution*, éditions Milan, Paris, 1996, p. 16.
80. NOR (Malika), *op. cit.* p. 54.

dent prostitution is a choice, more or less conditioned, but a rational choice nonetheless.

This choice, this possibility of leading this type of "double life", is undoubtedly facilitated by the Internet. According to Yann Reuzeau's analysis: "Today, many prostitutes start out on the Internet. Many of them would never have done so without this 'falsely' virtual opportunity [...] because the great novelty of the Internet is that it opens up this profession to absolutely anyone. A basic computer, an Internet connection, two/three photos, a solid 15 minutes, and voila, you're an escort[81]!" This voluntary, amateur prostitution is also the subject of her latest play - *Les Débutantes, prostituées en quelques clics* - starring Marion, a 19-year-old medical student who, to pursue her studies, occasionally prostitutes herself via the Internet.

"Occasional" students include

Among the "occasional" prostitutes are students[82]. It may seem surprising to find this group in prostitution. However, we know that this population is far from "rolling in it", and many students have a "job" alongside their university obligations[83]. What's more, the majority of jobs offered and compatible with

---

81. REUZEAU (Yann), *Les Débutantes - Prostituées en quelques clics*, play, 2006, performed from November 2006 to February 2007 at La Manufacture des Abbesses in Paris, seen January 18, 2007.

82. We use the term "student prostitutes" to refer to both male and female students who prostitute themselves alongside their studies.

83. According to the Observatoire de la vie étudiante (OVE): in France, 47% of students have a salaried job in addition to their studies, and 15% of them work at least 6 months a year, at least part-time. Today, 45,000 students are in serious or long-term poverty, and 225,000 are struggling to finance their studies. Source: PHILIBERT (Jean-Marc), "La prostitution gagne les bancs de la fac", *Le Figaro*, October 30, 2006, p. 11.

a student's timetable are still not very lucrative. As a result, it's not so surprising to think that "for a young person in a fragile economic situation, the temptation is great when you see the attraction of the sums at stake in this type of activity[84]".

To date, little serious research has been carried out on the subject of occasional prostitution, and, what's more, with students as actors. In fact, the subject of occasional student prostitution recently "came out of the closet", following an announcement by the SUD-Étudiant union during demonstrations against the Equal Opportunities Act in the spring of 2006. The media picked up on the story in autumn 2006. According to the various sources gathered on this subject, students who prostitute themselves do so essentially out of need for money and lack of time, in order to have a sufficiently profitable job at the same time as their studies. The media emphasize the economic precariousness of students and the ever-increasing cost of living. And let's not forget that France is in the midst of an election campaign. As a result, it's fashionable to draw politicians' attention to sensitive issues... and to make them look good. On the other hand, none of these sources refers to any study that would make it possible to measure the scale of the phenomenon. Similarly, no scientific research has yet been published on student prostitution. This lack of research aroused my curiosity and guided my choice of thesis. On the other hand, a sociological study on Internet prostitution is currently underway. This is a study conducted by Sylvie Bigot, currently a sociology PhD student, on "l'épanouissement sexuel des femmes à travers l'escorting" (women's sexual

---

84. SCHAFF (Christelle), *op. cit.* p. 140

fulfillment through escorting). Her work is not yet published, but she presented it at a conference last June[85]. Although not specifically aimed at students, this work contains a number of relevant elements.

My study focuses on *voluntary* (chosen) prostitution, carried out *independently* and *occasionally* by *female students* via the *Internet,* who call themselves "escorts[86]". All these elements contribute to making this a singular practice among the many faces of prostitution.

Working on "student prostitution via the Internet" involves coming up against a number of obstacles, first and foremost those specific to the topic, but also those of a practical nature[87]. This is what we're going to focus on in the next section.

1.2 Conditions and Conduct of the Survey

As a preamble, we will highlight the practical conditions under which my investigation took place, and the context in which the results were elaborated. This epistemological work

---

85. BIGOT (Sylvie), *op. cit.*

86. The majority of escorts are women. My study therefore focuses on female student escorts. I did, however, meet a student (boy) - a former street prostitute - who now uses the Internet to solicit. His practice differs from that of the student escorts, and therefore gives us a better idea of what makes the latter so special.

87. "Working on a form of deviant behavior raises many emotional and methodological problems." HUMPHREYS (Laud), *Le Commerce des pissotières - Pratiques homosexuelles anonymes dans l'Amérique des années 1960*, Paris XIII, Éditions La Découverte, 2007, p. 27.

seems to me to be important, as it reveals a number of elements which are not without consequence for the material gathered. In fact, several authors[88] emphasize the importance of describing the survey process and the conditions under which materials were obtained. On this subject, Stéphane Beaud and Florence Weber point out that "survey 'data' cannot be analyzed outside the context of their production[89]". This section, written in the first person singular, therefore sets out the "first milestones" for appreciating and apprehending the data and analyses obtained. We shall see what difficulties I encountered during the research, how they influenced my approach and what means I used to get round them.

While Olivier Schwartz knew, when he began his research on the workers of northern France, "that the most intimate layers of the private sphere [would] remain largely, if not totally, inaccessible to him[90]", I didn't expect to come up against this kind of obstacle. Some of my teachers had warned me that I was tackling "a sensitive subject", but this only reinforced my decision to work on the subject. As Laud Humphreys rightly says, "Can we exclude a priori certain areas of human behavior from any scientific study? Should sex, religion, suicide or

---

88. See in particular: BEAUD (Stéphane) and WEBER (Florence), *Guide de l'enquête de terrain - Produire et analyser des données ethnographiques*, Éditions La Découverte, Paris, 1998; FAVRET-SAADA (Jeanne), *Les mots, la mort, les sorts - Sorcellerie contemporaine dans le Bocage de l'Ouest*, Éditions Gallimard, 1977; HUMPHREYS (Laud), *op. cit. cit*; PINSON (Michel) and PINSON-CHARLOT (Monique), *Voyage en grande bourgeoisie - Journal d'enquête*, PUF, Paris, 2005 (2nd updated edition - 1st ed.: 1997); SCHWARTZ (Olivier), *Le Monde privé des ouvriers - Hommes et femmes du Nord*, PUF, Paris, 1990.

89. BEAUD (S.) and WEBER (F.), *op. cit.* p. 21.

90. SCHWARTZ (Olivier), *op. cit.* p. 35.

Survey Framework

any other sensitive subject for society be struck off the list of possible areas of investigation [...] when the police, the press and other guardians of the social (political) order are interested in them[91]?"

I have to admit, though, that I wanted to change the subject of my investigation when, in December, I still hadn't found a single piece of scientific writing on student prostitution. But the desire to work on this theme was stronger, and I persevered, not without difficulty.

1.2.1 *Choosing a site*

When working on a deviant practice[92], "the first problem we encounter is locating the people to carry out the research[93]". Therein lies the difficulty when dealing with a hidden practice...

Instructive disillusionment

A theme unknown to collectives and associations

When I chose my subject, I had in mind to carry out my investigations on the Nantes university campus. In particular, I plan to take advantage of the opportunity offered by my

---

91. HUMPHREYS (Laud), *op. cit.* p. 181-182.

92. The term "deviance" is to be understood here in the sociological sense. According to Goffman, deviance concerns people judged to be "outside the norm", having practices qualified as "outside the norm" by those who call themselves "normal". GOFFMAN (Erving), *Stigmate - Les usages sociaux des handicaps*, Les Éditions de Minuit, Paris, 1975.

93. HUMPHREYS (Laud), *op. cit.* p. 28.

internship site[94] and my status as an intern to cooperate with the SUMPPS[95]. Through this service, I hope to be put in touch with students who are prostitutes, who have prostituted themselves or who are considering it. However, I soon realize that they don't spontaneously turn to SUMPPS services. My meetings with the nurses and the doctor from the university medical unit were particularly enlightening. They gave me a better grasp of the particular context in which my research was taking place, and of the difficulties I was likely to encounter when working on prostitution. I understand, for example, that from a statistical point of view, student prostitution is marginal. In fact, according to the professionals who have been working at the SUMPPS in Nantes for the past ten years, only three students from the Nantes campus have told them about their prostitution. In this respect, I have undoubtedly over-represented this phenomenon (or its visibility), as well as the likelihood of university medicine encountering this type of problem. I also failed to consider the "barrier" of professional secrecy: SUMPPS staff are not allowed to communicate the identities of the students in question to a third party.

During this same period, I met with many organizations likely to help me in my research. I contacted several structures more or

---

94. From October 2006 to May 2007, I was an intern at the Nantes delegation of the Mouvement du Nid. The work of this abolitionist association is based on meeting prostitutes in prostitution zones (mainly on the streets), in their living environment and at drop-in centers, as well as supporting them in their efforts to reintegrate into society (in conjunction with specialized services). Le Nid is also involved in awareness-raising (particularly among secondary school students), information and prevention activities.

95. SUMPPS: Service universitaire de médecine préventive et de promotion de la santé.

less closely linked to the student world[96] and associations sensitive to the theme of prostitution[97]. Once again, these meetings enabled me to better understand the difficulties surrounding the subject of my research: none of these groups could help me in any concrete way, as none of them had been in contact with student prostitutes. During my interviews with these various partners, I realized that for most of them, prostitution in the student environment was - and still is today - an "enigma", a "new" phenomenon. At the time, no one seemed to have mastered the subject (extent of the phenomenon, practices, profiles of student prostitutes...)[98].

Student prostitution and hostess bars

So I thought I'd go straight to the places where, according to the press and the people I'd met, student prostitution takes place. I listed the various "hostess bars" (also known as "cork bars") in the Nantes area[99].

---

96. The SUD-Étudiant union (Nantes and Saint-Denis branches); the Nantes CROUS; the Angers SUMPPS; two student mutual insurance companies (LMDE and SMEBA), and the Nantes Family Planning organization.

97. Le Mouvement du Nid (Nantes delegation and national branch in Clichy); the "prostitution mission" set up by Médecins du Monde (in Nantes); the association d'Une Rive à l'autre (in Nantes); AIDES (in Angers).

98. It was on this occasion that the Nantes delegation of the Mouvement du Nid offered me an internship. Within this association, my work consists of questioning (by means of questionnaires) a certain number of students on the Nantes campus about what they know about prostitution, and how they use information. The aim of the survey was to find out what would be the most "appropriate" medium for talking to them, in a preventive context, about the prostitution system. To this end, I distributed 180 questionnaires to second-year psychology and medical students. I processed 138 of them (using Sphinx software), then analyzed the results.

99. See GARNIER (Antoine), "Le procès des bars à hôtesses de Nantes débute aujourd'hui", *Presse Océan Grand Nantes*, September 3, 2007, p. 4.

In addition to the reluctance expressed by the teacher to whom I submitted my idea, a number of other factors finally made me change my mind. First of all, I'm not really comfortable going into a hostess bar on my own. Secondly, as one of the professionals at the Nantes Family Planning explained to me, I don't fit the "typical profile of the customer who frequents these bars". In that case, how and on what criteria could I approach the population I'm interested in? What's more, I'm aware of the difficulty of keeping an employee on site and during working hours.

At this stage of the investigation, I'm somewhat at a loss. There doesn't seem to be any "suitable" terrain in which to begin and conduct my research in satisfactory conditions. I fear, as Stéphane Beaud mentions, that I have been carried away by "a taste for the picturesque and the exotic", and that I have underestimated the importance of accessibility to the field. But I'm too invested in this subject and too attached to it to abandon it.

Student prostitution and the Internet

So I decided to target my population using another "tool": the Internet. While I'm not exactly thrilled with this approach (I'm not familiar with the Net and prefer to deal with a "real field"), it at least has the advantage of being more "reassuring".

First, I randomly consult several *escort girl* websites, trying to spot whether any of the "Net prostitutes" mention that they are also students in their adverts. It's a tricky task, given the sheer number of ads online. So I made a first "selection", focusing on the ads of those who mentioned their student activity. Of the hundred or so ads I consulted, barely a dozen were explicitly labelled "student". I then widened my selection, this time focusing on a number of "clues" that might lead me to believe that the person in question is a student. First, I look at the escort's age (and only select those under 30); then her availability (evenings and weekends, to emphasize the occasional nature of her escort activity, while leaving time for her studies); her interests and hobbies; and finally, sometimes her photograph... But this process remains approximate and unreliable, as it relies solely on my intuitions and leaves too much to chance. Nonetheless, I note that a relatively large number of escort profiles match these criteria (although I don't specify whether they are actually students). Nevertheless, I decide to contact around twenty of the escorts in my selection via their blog or email linked to their advert. To do this, I send them a standard e-mail in which I introduce myself and honestly explain my approach: "I'm doing a study on student prostitution, and I'm asking you to come in for an interview so that you can tell me about yourself, your background...". To date, I have received no reply.

Despite the ineffectiveness of this procedure (no response, hence no contact), consulting these ads makes me aware, in a way, of the scale of the prostitution phenomenon via the Internet. I also note, among the supposed student escorts, a wide diversity of prostitute "profiles" and "services" on offer. I thus refocused my object of study - student prostitution via the Internet - and began to understand how it works and how it presents itself. For example, I'm learning to familiarize myself with the specific jargon of prostitution via the Internet[100], I'm discovering particular forms of presentation (ads, blogs,

---

100. See Appendix 2 for definitions of terms specific to Internet prostitution.

specialized sites...), and I'm getting an idea of the types of services on offer, the rates on the "market"... In short, I'm observing a new form of solicitation and prostitution (via the Internet) that differs from the solicitation of street prostitution, which I'm more familiar with, having analyzed it last year[101]. However, this "new form" covers a multitude of realities, student escorting being one of them.

At the same time, I regularly read a discussion forum on online prostitution on the Web[102]. On this forum, several messages from characters mention student prostitution.

For almost four months (from August to November), this reading was more the result of curiosity than real work. It wasn't until early December, when I met and interviewed a student who prostitutes herself through this forum, that the latter became my field of research.

---

101. As part of the "Migration, Ethnicity and Urban Diversity" course (taken at the Université de Montréal), I produced a dossier entitled *La prostitution des femmes immigrées en Occident - Un choix contraint.*

102. Generally speaking, a forum is defined as a discussion space on the Internet that operates asynchronously, like a public mailbox. It enables a group of people to exchange opinions and ideas on a particular subject. Discussions take place in the form of electronic message threads, with instant or delayed publication. This publication is often long-lasting, as messages, if not deleted by the forum author or moderator, are archived on the Web (so they can be read at any time by all Internet users). Each user can read the contributions of other participants and make his or her own contribution in the form of posts. While all Internet users can consult (read) the contributions of other forumers, it is often necessary to register with the community in order to participate (write/post) in discussions.

1.2.2 The Forum as a research field

Discover the Forum and discover a world...

Becoming familiar with speech

I discovered the[103] Forum in the summer of 2006, following a search on the Internet for information circulated by the SUD-Étudiant union. As I've already mentioned, I was somewhat puzzled by this information. So I decided to see if I could find out more about it. My first instinct is to launch a Web search. To do this, I enter the words *"student prostitution" in* the search engine, and the first link I get is a *topic*[104] on this Forum.

From this first "encounter" with the Forum, I remember being surprised by the "lightness" with which the theme of prostitution was approached. Indeed, the few messages I consulted conveyed a rather "sympathetic" vision of prostitution, or at any rate less "gloomy" than that more often and more widely disseminated by other sources[105]. Several testimonials, for example, express the "fulfilling" and "pleasant" nature of prostitution. I'm particularly interested in Céline's story (see box).

Up until mid-October, I was visiting the Forum from time to time, in a more or less superficial manner. At the time, the Forum was an "object" of curiosity, of which I was wary, and which

---

103. I deliberately use a capital letter to designate the forum on which I work, the Forum as a research field.

104. Topic: General subject of an online discussion on an Internet forum. Please refer to Appendix 3 for definitions of terms used on online discussion forums (terms explained are followed by an *).

105. Within my internship structure in particular - an association which, let me remind you, takes an abolitionist stance on prostitution.

I didn't know how to use for my research. I was observing how it worked, and remained rather sceptical about the discourse on prostitution, prostitutes and clients. This discourse, which I judge at the time to be too "mawkish", "upsets" me, because it doesn't echo what I know or imagine about prostitution.

Converting journalism into a scientific tool

At the end of October, I read the first article on student prostitution to be published in a major national daily,[106] highlighting the use of the Internet. This article lends credence to my research topic (in my eyes, but especially in the eyes of my professors) and gives it a certain scope: "since the journalist is interested, why not the sociologist[107]?"

At the end of November, the major media[108] (press and television) took up the subject. They described student prostitution as an occasional activity chosen by a number of young people facing financial difficulties, in particular to pay for higher education and rent. According to these different sources, the main motivation for students who engage in occasional prostitution is financial. Although this reason is also mentioned on the Forum, it does not appear to be the only reason put forward by forumers*.

---

106. PHILIBERT (Jean-Marc), *op. cit.*

107. HUMPHREYS (Laud), *op. cit.* p. 8.

108. On November 23, 2006, France 2's Envoyé spécial broadcast a report on "Les occasionnelles de la prostitution". The prostitution of two students (one in a hostess bar, the other via the Internet) was highlighted.

First contact with my land

- Céline: "I was a student at the Beaux-Arts, and one day, in a café, a man approached me, handsome, friendly, well-dressed. He asked me if I'd be willing to accompany him to an exhibition opening for a fee [...] At the time, I was broke, struggling between my studies and odd jobs. I called him back a few days later, and agreed to the exhibition, but no sex. I bought myself a pretty little dress at Tati, some stockings at Monoprix, recustomized some old shoes and when he came to pick me up, I could tell he thought I was beautiful. For several months, he paid me for soft evenings, often for exhibitions, with meals in restaurants afterwards... I knew the art world, I knew how to hold a lively conversation on the subject and I know he appreciated that. There was never any sex, just a very sensual closeness. Then one day, when he came to pick me up, he put a lot more money in my hand. I often said to myself [...] that this money connection certainly excited me, an unconfessed fantasy perhaps... He was married. He was gentle and sensitive. For him, after class, I'd transform myself from a cool baba student into a sexy, desirable young woman. [...] That was my short career as an escort girl. And even if you can put very ugly words on it - prostitution, deception, money - I know that he and I had a lovely story under contract... [...] [...]

- *Lise [in reply to Céline]: You're right, and if you've had a good time too, there's no harm in doing yourself good...*

- Céline: From my short career as an escort girl, I have a very exciting and troubled memory..., I certainly fulfilled a fantasy, giving myself for money, a troubled memory because it was with a very refined and very imaginative man and I discovered with him, to give him pleasure, some very very very... hard games [...]."

Following this media investment, which is sometimes directly inspired by elements of the[109] Forum, I read it more "actively". I'm beginning to identify the forumers, the general atmosphere, the tone of the speeches... and I'm trying to extract information (excerpts from discussions) that could be used for my research work. My use of the Forum is now taking a new turn: I'm no longer just a "curious" reader, as I'm now trying to immerse myself in this terrain. I've also noticed that my view of the Forum's discourse on prostitution has changed. The comments made on the Forum seem to me to be more "nuanced" than those I read the first few times.

"Be with[110]": becoming a forumeuse

To perfect my "impregnation" of the field, I want to become "active" and contribute to the Forum, to have visibility and therefore a place within this microcosm. So I'm becoming a forumer. However, I have no idea how I'm going to be welcomed by the other participants, or how I'm going to present myself. In fact, I'm still very wary and reticent about the sincerity of the testimonials on the Forum. On this type of terrain, we're in a completely different reality. The usual rules of communication are somewhat blurred: exchanges are written (no orality), indirect (no temporality), orchestrated by an intermediary (the computer), feelings and sentiments are signalled by *emoticons** (or *smileys**) and the speakers are not observable.

---

109. I recognize testimonials from forumers in several articles, including Bastien BONNEFOUS, "À la fac de la précarité, option tapin", *Le 20 Minutes*, November 23, 2006, p. 6.

110. WEBER (Florence), *Le Travail à côté*, INRA/EHESS éditions, Paris, 1989.

Learn the rules of the game

Nevertheless, I decided to register under my first pseudonym[111]. On this occasion, I changed my name and disguised
myself as "a fourth-year medical student living in Paris". The
Forum is a world that's foreign to me. I'm groping my way in,
and this disguise feels like a cover. It also shows me how easy it
is, in this type of communication, to "fool" and invent a story, a
character...

Under this first pseudonym, I *post** several remarks. This first
experience enabled me to understand that the Forum is governed
by rules. Indeed, after posting a question on the subject of
respondents' relationship with their bodies, a forumer takes me
back and reminds me that there are certain times for dialogue
on such and such a subject, and that it would be a good idea to

---

111. To be able to participate in discussions and access the various forum
features. When registering, the new forumer chooses a pseudonym, a confi-
dential password and an avatar (optional). They then provide a number of
personal details (some of which are optional) to define their "profile" ("user
profile"). If the forumer wishes, he or she can complete the profile with a
"Chinese portrait". This option provides more details about your personal
life (hobbies, passions, interests...). They can also create a "personal space",
where they can add photographs, website links, blogs, etc. These details are
not fixed: the forumer can modify them as they wish, having entered their
"password" beforehand, and they can be consulted by all Internet users.
Once registration is complete, a forum function systematically completes the
profile of the "new forumer" by adding his or her forum registration date.
The new forumer now has the keys to participate in the various discussions
(replying in general or to a particular message) and to contact other forumers
via "mp" (i.e. "personal message").

respect them[112]. I also learn that conventions dictate the use of appropriate language. In my message, I wrote "sell your body" to refer to prostitution. The forumer's intervention underlines my "clumsiness" and corrects what I said - "you don't sell your body but a sexual service and a moment of intimacy" - showing me that there is an "appropriate" language for prostitution. So it's a good idea for me to spot the "indigenous language[113]", and use it wisely in my next *posts**. Lightness does not prevent a certain amount of control. Another misunderstanding makes me realize that it's necessary to be attentive to the sensitivities of others, as

---

112. In addition to this informal "self-regulation" (which comes from users), there are often internal rules that formally govern the use that can be made of the forum. Indeed, many forums require acceptance of a charter* prior to participation. On the Forum, this charter, drawn up by one of the Forum's four moderators*, can be found at the top of the discussion threads*, on the first page. It describes the roles and functions of the moderators and moderators of the site's various forums, and explains how to contact them "if necessary". It goes on to explain that any message containing "racist, anti-Semitic, xeno-phobic, insulting or defamatory remarks, [...] advertisements [as well as] personal contact details, names and/or contact details of practitioners" will be systematically deleted; and adds that "the prostitution forum is not intended to display advertisements from professionals or good deals from customers, but to open up debate" [written in bold in the charter]. The charter concludes with a greeting to participants.Another thread posted by the moderator (entitled "Reminder on how the forum works") reinforces the rules set out in the charter and specifies a few features such as: the ban on "quoting the names and contact details of hotels on the forum, but [authorization] to exchange this information by private message or e-mail"; "publishing texts written in mp, with or without information on the pseudonyms concerned [on pain of seeing these messages] systematically deleted without explanation"; or the fact of asking the moderators "if you [participants] feel that the moderation time is too long and if you notice trollish* or off-topic messages". As a forumer, I've found that off-topic* messages are quickly deleted by the moderator. Before being permanently deleted, these messages are flooded* and "threatened" by Forum regulars*.

113. WEBER (Florence), *op. cit.*

in any research field. In this context, the Forum is indeed a place where social practices and interactions linked to prostitution are played out. Thus, "from the moment I discovered the place of 'action', I knew that the subjects of my research would be to be found there[114]".

A fragile investigative position

A few days after registering under the first pseudonym, I decide to change strategy and opt for the "truth". My aim is to establish "regular communication" with the Forum's student prostitutes, in order to "build a closeness with [these] subjects [and] enter into a relationship with them that gives access to the intimate[115]".

I open a topic[116] under a new pseudonym[117] and create a new e-mail address at the same time. This time, I introduce myself as a sociology student who's doing a dissertation on student prostitution and wants to collect testimonials from students who prostitute themselves. Under this pseudonym, the tone and content of my messages are more in line with my own. My first intervention is clear and sober, without being too formal. I mustn't forget that I'm talking to students, i.e. people who, in a way, resemble me. I therefore find it appropriate to adopt a

---

114. HUMPHREYS (Laud), *op. cit.* p. 28.

115. SCHWARTZ (Olivier), *op. cit.* p. 36.

116. The Forum is organized into *discussion threads* (or *topics*). An initial message launches a new thread. Each new reply to this implicitly chronological thread opens a new discussion thread, as a reply to a previous message. All these threads are often grouped into themes.

117. I have chosen a pseudonym where I can be identified as a woman (common feminine noun), but unlike the majority of female prostitutes on the Forum, my pseudonym is in no way "racy".

simple discourse and use humor to have a certain "closeness" with the respondents. Similarly, I try to "play the game" of communication via a forum and use *smileys**. Finally, I try to appear friendly and open to discussion[118].

Under this pseudonym, I voluntarily decide not to intervene in the other topics to mark that my role on the Forum is not to debate nor to expose my ideas and points of view, but to meet prostituted students of the Forum. I've kept to this line of conduct throughout the survey, for two main reasons. The first ties in with Olivier Schwartz's concern to "limit the effects of censorship that my presence inevitably triggers in the respondents[119]". The second reason is that I'm afraid my interventions might be misinterpreted, which could do me a disservice. I'm aware, however, that this posture will prevent me from creating links with certain forumers, as not everyone will necessarily read my topic. In this case, my "visibility" is necessarily limited.

---

118. His precautions seem essential to generate discussion. On the Forum, you need to have a certain "know-how" and abide by the implicit rules of the community (the explicit rules - set out in the charter - should be taken for granted). By "know-how" I mean mastery of the "forum tool": technical skills, but also intellectual skills (mastery of the forumer's jargon, but also that specific to this forum in particular). On the Forum, participants appreciate posts that are written "correctly", i.e. without too many spelling mistakes, without too many abbreviations, that proscribe "sms" writing, that have a clear presentation (by skipping lines, for example), and embellished with smileys. As far as the tone of the message is concerned, it's best to use courteous language and appropriate vocabulary, preferably not vulgar (for example, the term "whore" is frowned upon by newcomers). Likewise, tolerance and open-mindedness towards each other's testimonials are two recommended principles for gaining acceptance in the community.

119. SCHWARTZ (Olivier), *op. cit.* p. 47.

Survey Framework

Shortly after my topic went online, several forumers encouraged me in my approach, without however applying to meet me. I think I can now find my place on the Forum.

But these positive reactions were followed by more hostile ones. Indeed, a few hours after the launch of my topic, a new forumer, also presenting herself as a student (not a prostitute), took advantage of my thread to ask questions. The initial subject of the discussion shifted to a debate between this new forumer and the regulars[120]. As a result of this "newcomer's" interventions, I'm "suspected" by several forumers of not being a student, but rather an e-journalist. This animosity is due to recent articles and reports broadcast in the country, and predisposes forumers to a certain distrust.

At first glance, being neither a prostitute nor a client, my arrival on this Forum doesn't seem all that justified. "How can you be in a world without being in it[121] ?" Faced with this atmosphere, I try to justify my presence on the Forum, my intentions and my approach, and explain what distinguishes sociology from journalistic investigation. I'm careful to remain sincere and

---

120. The Forum's regulars form the "community of forumers", who bring the Forum to life and shape it. To become part of this community, you need to be recognized and accepted by the regulars. This integration can only be effective if the new participant integrates the Forum's norms and practices.One of the ways (and probably the most effective) of gaining recognition and a place in the community of forumers is to create affinities with participants, if possible with those who are already well known in the group. These links are forged gradually, as discussions and messages are exchanged. The more you're present on the forum and receptive to other people's messages/interventions, the more likely you are to build a relationship with group members. But posting regularly isn't enough: you also need to make sure that your contributions are noticed and, above all, appreciated by others.

121. HUMPHREYS (Laud), *op. cit.* p. 37.

moderate in what I say, and try to appear credible and sympathetic. I then understand that while it's not difficult to "approach the milieu", i.e. the Forum, nor to "make contact" with forumers, "the real problem [is] to maintain this contact[122]".

The fact that I'm suspected of "bad intentions" does, however, offer me the opportunity to "find a role, a function that makes [the researcher] useful to the group without necessarily sharing their practices[123]". Indeed, by guaranteeing anonymity and a neutral, objective discourse, I become worthy of interest, even useful. I become "the one who will break out of the clichés" and, in so doing, restore their image.

This will not be my only test. In the course of the investigation, I will have to demonstrate my good faith on several occasions[124].

Recommendation principle[125]

The first forumers to agree to help me were clients of prostitutes. A *former forumer** sends me a "mp"[126] in which he offers me his help. As he's well known and recognized in the forum community, I think he'll be able to use his influence with the Forum's student prostitutes to convince them to meet me. Like Michel Pinson and Monique Pinson-Charlot, I'm well aware of how "personal recommendation is a necessity to

---

122. HUMPHREYS (Laud), *ibid.* p. 34.

123. HUMPHREYS (Laud), *ibid.* p. 37.

124. Before recommending me to a Forum student escort, a forumer is waiting for me to prove to him that I really am a sociology student. So I e-mail him a photograph of my student card, taking care to hide my first and last names as well as my photograph.

125. PINSON (Michel) and PINSON-CHARLOT (Monique), *op. cit.*

126. On discussion forums, mp ("personal messages") are messages that can only be read by the author and recipient of the message.

obtain the principle of the[127] interview". I'll be using it to get the following appointments[128].

But word of mouth isn't always enough. With no new offers and on the strength of my first interview, I try another tactic. On my own initiative (i.e. without a recommendation), I send PMs to forumers I identify as student prostitutes[129]. At the time, there were five of them (all girls). All the students I contact via mp decline my proposal: either because they don't feel like it, or because they don't have the time. From their responses (for those who have replied), I sense that any insistence on my part

---

127. PINSON (Michel) and PINSON-CHARLOT (Monique), *op. cit.* p. 21.

128. I mainly met student escorts. I also conducted interviews with clients of occasional escorts - some of whom are also students - as well as an interview with a student (boy) - a former street prostitute - who now uses the Internet to solicit. His experience of prostitution on the street and his distance from it - he's been a prostitute for over three years - shed light on the specific features of each type of prostitution, particularly Internet prostitution.

129. The Forum is regularly updated with new pseudonyms, which arrive in varying numbers at different times. However, a new pseudonym does not necessarily mean a new person. In fact, a real person can have several pseudonyms to their credit (known as multi-pseudo*) and present themselves under distinct identities. This type of procedure is "frowned upon" by many forumers, who see in it a certain dishonesty. In fact, they often discuss it among themselves. When a forumer suspects a pseudonym, he refers it to another he knows and trusts to try and unmask the multi-pseudonym. During a meeting between forumers, for example, I learned of a client forumer who had another pseudonym under which he presented himself as a student escort. Under his escort pseudonym, he contacts certain forum escorts via mp, befriending them in order to extract personal information from them. The JAD* (forumers' meeting) is an opportunity to check that a pseudonym really corresponds to a person, and that what he says on the Forum echoes reality. I've noticed that forumers are sensitive to this type of "deception": they don't want to be fooled. This no doubt stems from the fact that the subject of prostitution leads forumers to open up and confide in each other... something they're not used to doing in front of their loved ones.

will result in a refusal[130]. Two of them, however, offer me an alternative: they agree to answer my questions, provided they do so via the Internet. I negotiate to convince them to meet, insisting on the advantages of this approach. But in view of their reluctance, I finally agreed to send them a "questionnaire" via the Internet[131]. This process takes around two months: I wait for the first series of questions to be returned before sending out the next one (which involves five round-trips). Of the two respondents, only one plays the game through to the end. The other only returned two series, and despite regular reminders, she hasn't been in touch since.

A new stage: the collective meeting

In addition to the Forum and the interviews, I was able to meet around twenty forumers[132] at a JAD[133]. This organized

---

130. I recognize myself in what Olivier SCHWARTZ wrote when he asked workers to be interviewed; *op. cit.*, p. 39.

131. My ambition is to obtain a written testimony as rich as one gathered during an interview. My fear is that, with this system, the respondent will limit himself to the questions formulated and answer them succinctly. To remedy this problem, the proposed support must be sufficiently precise ("closed") for the respondent to understand correctly, but sufficiently open ("free") for him to express himself widely. I therefore set out to convert my interview grid into a kind of "open questionnaire", to adapt it to this type of procedure. To do this, I split the questionnaire into several themes, each comprising a series of questions. I also adapt the way I write my questions so that they lend themselves to oral reading. As a result, the wording is less formal (I'm on first-name terms), and I sometimes use humor and colloquialisms. Finally, I decide to send the series of questions "step by step", i.e. theme by theme. This way, I believe, respondents will be more encouraged to answer at length.

132. During the afternoon, I met a total of: 10 customers (all men), 9 Internet prostitutes - including 1 boy (with a male clientele) and 3 student escorts (2 of whom I interviewed).

133. *JAD (Just a dream)*: (real) meeting between Forum participants.

Survey Framework

meeting between forumers offers me several useful elements for the survey. Firstly, it allows me to participate in new forms of social exchange and interaction. I talk for varying lengths of time with some of the forumers. We talk about their prostitution practices and how they see it, they ask me about my research work, we talk about "life on the Forum"... In this respect, I can see how attached and involved the forumers are in the Forum. According to them, the Forum is "much more than just a place for discussion", "it's a place to live! The JAD is also an opportunity for me to assert my position as a researcher in the eyes of certain forumers who still had doubts about my intentions. Last but not least, this collective encounter enabled me to "verify" - in a more concrete way - the information gathered through the Forum about the respondents. By seeing them and talking to them, I capture more details about their identities - identities which, incidentally, are easier to "verify" than through the written word.

Following the JAD, several participants post friendly comments about me on the Forum, and some send me messages of encouragement. As a result, my place in this space became more visible, and I was increasingly asked to take part in the various online discussions. It was also following this collective encounter that a forumer invited me to take part in another forum, also on the subject of prostitution.

Despite the obstacles encountered in gathering the material necessary for my study - no direct contact possible with and in the field, a sensitive and little-known subject - which led me to use an Internet discussion forum as a means of meeting my respondents, I was nevertheless able to gather testimonies from escorts and customers. In the next section, we'll look at what distinguishes student escorts from other prostitutes, particularly in terms of how they conceive and approach their practice. Then, in the third section, we'll try to gain a better understanding of what leads some students to choose prostitution, by highlighting the different forms of rupture that run through their life stories.

PART TWO:

STUDENT PROSTITUTES ONLINE:

IN A CLASS ALL THEIR OWN?

Ordinary students

Working on students as a social group is no easy task, since the term covers a multitude of profiles and realities. Certainly, certain key characteristics remain - youth of the group, exceptional availability of time, autonomy in the making, etc. - but today, among young people pursuing higher education, diversity outweighs homogeneity. This diversity is the result of the gradual generalization of studies beyond the baccalaureate[1], underlining the transition from the time of the "heirs[2]" to that of the mass university. If all those enrolled in higher education

---

1. GALLAND (Olivier) and OBERTI (Marco), *Les Étudiants*, Éditions La Découverte, Paris, 1996, p. 3.

2. BOURDIEU (Pierre) and PASSERON (Jean-Claude), *Les Héritiers: les étudiants de la culture*, éditions de Minuit, Paris, 1964.

are taken into account, their numbers represent more than half of the 18-22 age group[3]. In this context, the "student" category brings together people from a wide range of educational levels and social backgrounds, with equally varied practices, lifestyles and ambitions.

The students in the survey are no exception. This "group" is heterogeneous in a number of ways. Firstly, in terms of variables such as gender, age, type of higher education and type of institution attended, level of study and marital status; and secondly, in terms of their living conditions - in relation to their social environment of origin - and the way in which they live their lives as students. However, all correspond to the "typical model" of the student described by Béduwé and Épinasse in their study on "student populations[4]". This model accounts for 80% of university enrolments, and includes students under the age of 27 (after which they are no longer eligible for certain tax and social benefits) who have continued their higher education without interruption. Likewise, the students I met and interviewed have several points in common. They could, for example, be mistaken for law, economics or science students, notably in the way they present themselves and the way they dress[5]. What's more, they

---

3. Enrolment growth was particularly strong after the mid-1990s; BEAUD (Stéphane), *80 % au bac et après?*, Éditions La Découverte, Paris, 2003.

4. GALLAND (Olivier) and OBERTI (Marco), *op. cit.* p. 17; Original source: BÉDUWÉ (C.) and ÉPINASSE (J.-M.), *"L'université et ses publics"*, *Éducation et Formations*, 40, March 1995, p. 33-46.

5. Within the university environment, there are different groups of students with a certain "dress code", depending on their course of study. Generally speaking, students in the humanities and social sciences can be identified by their "bohemian style", while students in law, economics and science tend to wear dark-colored, soberly cut clothes without too many accessories. At the time of the interviews, the respondents looked more like the latter.

share a common characteristic: they belong to the category - also highly diverse - of prostitutes.

"Stand out[6]"

The respondents are driven by a desire - more or less conscious - to distinguish themselves from other social categories, in various aspects of their lives. This desire, which had already become apparent to me through their various contributions to the Forum, was confirmed during the interviews. First, we'll look at how the interviewees distinguish themselves from their original social milieu, and then examine what sets them apart from other prostitutes[7].

2.1 STUDIES AND DISTINCTION

The respondents come from both working and middle-class backgrounds, with the exception of one from the upper classes. Their parents are, for the most part, unqualified. Their professions are at the bottom of the social hierarchy (such as sales clerk, secretary, nursery assistant, etc.) and/or they are in precarious situations (long-term unemployment, invalidity, etc.).

Unlike their parents, the respondents are in higher education and are - or soon will be - graduates. The cultural baggage

---

6. The use of the term "distinguish" is not insignificant. It is used here in reference to the concept of "distinction" described by Pierre Bourdieu in his book *La Distinction - Critique sociale du jugement*. Distinguishing oneself implies "a break with the ordinary attitude towards the world which, given the conditions of its accomplishment, is a social break", *ibid.* p. 5.

7. We remind you that the term "prostitutes" refers to both female and male prostitutes, but by convention we use the feminine form.

Student Prostitutes Online: In a Class All their Own?

provided by their schooling and the fact of graduating enable students to rise in the social hierarchy, and occupy a more valued and esteemed place than their parents. They are well aware of the stakes involved, and of the gap that is emerging - and which seems to widen as the level of education rises - between them and their original social milieu. In this regard, Anne-Sophie - an only child, whose parents are office workers, and who is currently in her first year of science at university - declares ironically: "I'm raising the family standard just with my baccalaureate!"

2.1.1 Education and social background

Through their studies, the respondents set their sights on professions with "power" - economic, intellectual and symbolic - that are highly valued socially. Julien, whose mother was a nurse, wants to "do international trade"; Ambre, whose father stopped at primary school and whose mother at secondary school, aspires to teach at university; Claire, brought up in a family of shopkeepers "in the middle of nowhere", is currently finishing her biology thesis. As a result, their social ascension is significant, and the distinction from their original environment is noticeable. This social ascent - facilitated by the democratization of higher education[8] and the entry of the school preoccupation into all

---

8. The evolution of industrial societies is characterized by an undeniable reduction in inequality of educational opportunity - at secondary school level on the one hand and, to a more relative extent, at higher education level on the other. Although this reduction in inequality of opportunity is significant, it should not obscure the fact that inequalities remain high. In BOUDON (Raymond), *L'Inégalité des chances - La mobilité sociale dans les sociétés industrielles*, Éditions Armand Colin, Paris, 1979, p. 149.

social milieus - is among other things the result of a "thirst for learning" combined with the desire to "become somebody".

A taste for school

In the lives of the respondents, school and studies occupy a relatively important place. For some, "vacations were always too long!", for others "school is nothing but good memories... apart from maths!" In any case, all of them show a definite interest in educational institutions, and reveal the pleasure they had and still have in learning. The testimony of Ambre - who has just obtained her Master's degree in Literature and is currently preparing for the CAPES - illustrates this idea very well: "I've always loved studying... I still do! [...] and when I become a teacher, I'll prepare for the agrégation and probably even a doctorate."

In fact, most of the people we interviewed have had a "care-free" school career [where] everything has gone smoothly. Some, like Claire - from a middle-class background and currently doing her PhD in biology - have even had an exemplary education. In this regard, Claire declares that her schooling has always gone "very, very well! I've always been the best, quite a model student, you know? [...] So my career path was more like top of the class! I was very easy, I wasn't a hard worker, but once I was in front of my copy, I found a way to succeed. I had an average of 17 in my A-levels, spent 2 years in a smart Parisian preparatory school and got good results, working less than the others... I passed, got my DEA, so Master 2, was ranked third and got a scholarship. In principle, it's a sort of merit-based scholarship. And now I'm doing my thesis!

However, those who escape the rule of success do not give up their quest for social recognition. For example, Anne-Sophie - 21 years old and currently in her first year of science studies - has twice failed the entrance exam to a Grande Ecole. Nevertheless, this underscores the fact that she shares the same desire for social recognition as the other interviewees: despite the difficulties, and despite her parents' discouragement[9], she has chosen to embark on a "prestigious" course of study. At the time of our meeting in February 2006, Anne-Sophie had just completed her first semester at university, but had decided to reorient her studies towards a school to become a nursery nurse. This prospect makes her optimistic: "I've always wanted to do something related to the medical field [...] and now, with the nursery school, I'll definitely be a nursery nurse! I'll have a job I like, that's for sure! In a way, this decision relativizes the failure she suffered in the entrance exam to the Grande École, because, given her social background and considering her future profession - nursery nurse - Anne-Sophie is on the way up the social ladder.

For these middle- and working-class young people, school is seen as a means of "escaping one's condition", a social elevator. It offers them the opportunity to become and be "someone[10]".

"Become somebody!"

For these students, whose parents have no qualifications and have experienced or are experiencing unemployment

---

9. In this regard, Anne-Sophie declares that her parents felt that "she had thought too big" by committing herself to a Grande Ecole training program.
10. BEAUD (Stéphane), *op. cit.*

and/or financial difficulties, studying is a "guarantee" for their future. Thanks to their qualifications, they can look forward to a "better" future, or at any rate one that is "more secure" than that of their parents. Throughout the interviews, all the respondents declared - more or less explicitly - their desire to "become someone". This expression implies several aspects: on the one hand, the aspiration to social recognition, and on the other, the desire for a certain comfort of life - linked to financial stability.

Academic and professional success is important to our interviewees. In this respect, Sandrine - whose mother is a nursery assistant (ADSEM) and whose father, an ex-retail worker, has been unemployed for six years - declares: "when I'm older, I'll be paid to be an architect, and that's the thing I most want to do in the world! From this point of view, the studies and professional future to which the respondents aspire remain their priority. Moreover, they recognize themselves first and foremost as students, and claim this status. They are proud of it, particularly in view of the "road travelled": "I'm proud of it [my studies], I came from a backwater and I did brilliant, super-elite studies...", confides Claire. This personal pride is amplified by the feeling that most of their success came from themselves: "They [her parents] were always proud of me, but they didn't influence my choices, I chose everything on my own, I did everything on my own...", says Claire. Claire's comments must be qualified, however, as we know that a certain number of objective conditions - democratization of schooling, family effort, state aid, etc. - also play a part in individual success. Willpower alone is not always enough to succeed. On the other hand, her speech shows that she expects recognition for her success, having had the merit of achieving it alone, despite conditions - given her family situation - less favorable than for children from the upper classes.

The professional future for which the respondents have set their sights means they can look forward to favorable, if not very favorable, living conditions. While some had doubts about the immediacy of landing a job as soon as they had obtained their diploma, they remained serene and confident about the prospects of their studies: "[...] And I tell myself that I'm lucky too, that my future prospects are pretty good! That in the studies I'm doing, normally there's no failure at the stage I'm at, and there's no unemployment in the profession itself, so..." (Sandrine). (Sandrine); "I'll definitely have a job! [...] What's more, where I'm going isn't blocked, there's demand!" (Anne-Sophie). In this context, and in contrast to what they experienced within their families, the respondents are assured of a certain financial stability enabling them "to live in peace", i.e. to enjoy a comfortable lifestyle "without worrying too much about expenses", and without having to give up certain projects for lack of financial means.

2.1.2 Studies and a new peer group

For a number of students, entering higher education is an opportunity to leave the family home, sometimes even their home town or region, and learn to live more independently. These changes lead them to make new acquaintances and friends, creating new networks and peer groups. It's also an opportunity to rub shoulders with young people whose backgrounds and lifestyles differ from their own.

"We're not from the same world!"

For any young person from a working or middle-class background, joining a prestigious training program - such as a Grande École - is an opportunity to enter "a new world": that of the ruling classes[11].

In this "new world", students may feel "apart" or "out of step" with their classmates, particularly in terms of their experiences, tastes, hobbies and interests. Sandrine - who, after passing her baccalauréat, went on to enroll in a preparatory class for a Grande École - explains, for example, that she sometimes felt like "the alien of the class", because, in her opinion, her classmates didn't have "the same vision of the world". However, it's clear that students use strategies - more or less consciously - to find the keys to their place in the group. Claire talks about this quite lucidly: "I went to state schools, popular schools... Until première, I was in an ordinary lycée in the provinces, where you had to criticize the teachers and be rubbish to have friends. I was top of the class... In my final year, I went to the French lycée in Berlin, a semi-private lycée with a fairly high class of children from "good families", sons and daughters of diplomats, bankers... It changed me! And then my teachers pushed me to go to Paris to study at an elitist lycée, an engineering school... Children of teachers or engineers, well brought up... And here I was, in the middle of it all! But it was all right, I made my place...". One strategy, for example, is to adopt certain practices and habits of the dominant group. This may involve cultural outings, or the

---

11. Bourdieu (Pierre), *La Noblesse d'état - Grandes écoles et esprit de corps*, Les éditions de Minuit, Paris, 1989.

Student Prostitutes Online: In a Class All their Own?

way they dress or express themselves[12]... As far as Claire and Sandrine are concerned, they both admit to having discovered several practices, thanks to their new friends, that they now share with them. Claire, for example, gently scoffs at her friends' attraction to opera, before adding "but it's true that it's great all the same!" Then she continues: "I can't make generalizations about people [her friends] who are all different... Let's just say that my friends from my engineering school, they didn't grow up... at least for the most part, in the same environment as me... They don't know divorce or cheating, or sex outside of a love story. But for example, none of us smokes, we don't drink much, and we're rather 'well-behaved'. My father is much more extroverted and does more crazy things than all his friends put together..."

It's worth noting that in her speech, Claire includes herself and her friends: "we're pretty wise", and contrasts what she experienced in her family environment with her current reality. This shows the extent to which the initial differences experienced by students from less privileged backgrounds when rubbing shoulders with students from more affluent families are fading, and that the reference group is now the one with whom they share, to this day, the same ways of living[13].

Being deserving

On the whole, students enrolled in classes préparatoires and Grandes Écoles work at a relatively fast pace, with fairly

---

12. BOURDIEU (Pierre), *op. cit.*
13. ERNAUX (Annie), *La Place*, Gallimard, Paris, 1983.

"demanding" schedules[14]. What's more, as the competition is "tough", they need to work "seriously" if their ambition is to "stand out from the crowd". The students therefore devote a good part of their time to their studies. In fact, Sandrine declares that during her "two years of prep school", she "hardly went out at all", "to be able to work and succeed". For young people from middle-class backgrounds, success in "this environment" takes on a particular tone. It takes on an air of "battle" and "revenge" against their more modest origins. In the words of Claire and Sandrine, we perceive a certain "contempt" for their fellow graduates, most of whom come from the upper classes. In their view, the latter "deserve less credit" for ending up at a Grande École, since "thanks to their origins", they possess "all the keys to success". It is precisely against these "keys", i.e. the "advantages" - in terms of economic, cultural and social capital - enjoyed by the upper classes in general that Claire and Sandrine rebel. Both point to a number of "shortcomings" and social handicaps - cultural heritage - vis-à-vis their peers, which they have to overcome if they are to succeed. Students from less privileged backgrounds have to "fight" to "earn their place" and thus prove to others - classmates, but also their families - that their place in this training is legitimate and "amply deserved". As a result, they have to redouble their efforts - by working harder, for example - to show that they are capable of succeeding in a world that is not, *a priori,* their own.

---

14. According to a survey of students in the Alpes-Maritimes, students in preparatory classes spend 45.2 hours a week on university work, compared with 22 hours for language students and 35.1 hours for science students. GALLAND (Olivier) and OBERTI (Marco), *op. cit.* p. 42; Original source: CHENU *et al, La Vie étudiante dans les Alpes-Maritimes,* GERM/Université de Nice, 1993.

These points show just how crucial studies and schooling in general are in the lives of our respondents. The institution of school offers them the "hope" of "becoming someone", and they all intend to seize this opportunity to escape their original social milieu.

2.2 HIGH-CLASS PROSTITUTES?

These students therefore differ from their families, but also in their practice of prostitution. Indeed, in the collective imagination, the figure embodied by the prostitute most often echoes a woman whose life is marked by a painful past and who, "to overcome sexual intercourse with a client, takes drugs or gets drunk, thus inflicting additional violence on herself[15]". In all cases, the social gaze contributes to making prostitutes outcasts, deviants. Student prostitutes[16] don't seem to fit this profile. They are people with a certain cultural background and plans for the future. What's more, they are socially integrated and recognized as such: they have a recognized and valued activity (studying), friends, family... in other words, a social life outside prostitution. As a result, student prostitutes, by virtue of their student status (and all that this entails), seem to stand out in the prostitution arena.

Student escorts also differ in the very nature of their prostitution, as well as in the way they approach and view it.

---

15. SCHAFF (Christelle), *Prostitution en France : l'enquête*, Éditions de la Lagune, 2007, p. 73.

16. By convention, we use the term "prostitutes" to refer to all prostitutes (women and men), "student prostitutes" to refer to students (women and men) who prostitute themselves while studying, and "student escorts" to refer to our female respondents who prostitute themselves via the Internet.

As we saw in the first part of this study, prostitution has many faces, reflecting very different realities. As far as student prostitution is concerned, Guy Parent - head of the brigade de répression du proxénétisme - explains that it is "very difficult to quantify the phenomenon [because] students[17] escape the traditional circuits of the profession. [What's more,] they are very discreet and by definition only work occasionally[18]". In his view, student escorts "don't belong to a network" and mainly find their clients via the Internet, "either with more or less explicit escort girl ads, or on more traditional dating sites [...][19]". However, "traditional prostitution", i.e. - to use Guy Parent's words - that which comes under the "classic circuits", brings together "professional" prostitutes, whether independent or not, who most often solicit on the street. It is in relation to this type of prostitution that occasional student escorting stands out.

In our study, one respondent stands out from the others:

Julien, street prostitute for two years

Julien - the only male student prostitute in the survey - whose prostitutional practices differ from those of the women interviewed. While all of them are referred to as "escorts", Julien describes himself more as a "prostitute", or even a "whore": "I'm, well, it's true, I'm a whore and that's it! I'm a whore! Moreover, while all of them contact their clients via the Internet, Julien's

---

17. Note that Guy Parent is talking about female student *prostitutes,* and in no way refers to male prostitution.

18. AHMED-CHAOUCH (Azzedine), "Elles se prostituent pour financer leurs études", *Aujourd'hui en France,* January 1st, 2007, p. 14.

19. AHMED-CHAOUCH (Azzedine), *ibid.*

prostitution practice remains closer to the traditional form than to the escorting practiced by his female counterparts. As a result, Julien's reality provides a better understanding of the specificities of each type of prostitution, and thus highlights what makes female student escorts so special. It therefore seems appropriate to give an account of Julien's experience.

I contact Julien on the advice of Anne-Sophie - a student escort interviewed a month earlier. Before meeting, we communicate by mp for about a month.

We meet after class on the metro platform. Julien presents himself as a "classic" student: he's wearing jeans, a jogging jacket and has his course bag on his back. Outwardly, he looks younger than his years. He's beardless, rather slim and has a rather soft voice. We sit down in a café and chat for a while before starting the interview, as Julien looks uncomfortable. He's nervous, keeps to himself and says he's not sure he can answer the questions, as he's "not used to talking about it [his prostitution] like that". During the interview, Julien rarely elaborates on his answers. Some of what he says is "crude", and his experience of prostitution differs from what escorts have told me before. I notice that throughout the interview, I adopt a very empathetic attitude towards him. Following the interview, we continue to communicate on the Forum, and Julien provides me with new information about his prostitution[20].

At the age of 19, Julien begins his life as a university student, living alone with his maternal great-aunt since the death of his mother four years earlier. Julien has never lived with his father, and has had no contact with him since the age of 7. Nor does he know his paternal family. Julien describes himself as a "loner"

---

20. Here's an extract from one of Julien's messages, written three months after our interview: "Since we met, I've been going out with my clients, one to tell you the truth, to the restaurant with my client at Trocadéro, I charged him as if it were a pass, and then he paid me extra for the little I stayed with him. I also gave a massage to another customer, and discovered that I was good at massaging, lol [I laugh]! even though it was the first time I'd ever done it [...]."

who "doesn't feel the need to have friends". He does, however, have a friend - whom he met in high school - with whom he "sometimes chats on msn[21] as she lives in Australia", as well as his great-aunt whom he considers as such: "she's like my friend [...] she's very open".

Julien started prostituting himself at the age of 16, while still in high school. For more than two years, he regularly - several times a week - went to the Porte Dauphine[22] to solicit. In doing so, he obeyed the rules and practices of street prostitution: each evening, Julien made between three and five passes and collected between 150 and 300 euros.

According to him, "the death of [his] mother turned everything upside down". He explains that this event "turned him upside down" and that "that's why [he] went into it [prostitution]". It's obvious that an event such as the death of a loved one leaves its mark on a person's life, especially when it's the only parent you have left. At 15, an age when you're still heavily dependent on your family, Julien found himself alone, or almost alone. True, he lives with his great-aunt, with whom he "gets on well", but she's no substitute for the authority and role of a mother. In fact, his great-aunt is more "permissive" and "out of touch" than Julien's mother ever was. She doesn't ask him any questions when he's away three or four nights a week, and seems content with her grand-nephew's justifications: "I'd tell her I was going to a friend's house, and that was it... she'd let me[23]".

At the start of his practice, prostitution was for Julien a kind of "refuge" from a reality he found hard to accept. He couldn't bear the idea of having been "powerless" in the face

---

21. *msn* = instant messaging on the Internet.

22. The Porte Dauphine in Paris, near the Bois de Boulogne, is known as a major prostitution area. The area is divided, with each "sector" corresponding to a particular type of prostitution. These include male, transvestite and transsexual prostitution.

23. When Julien was a street prostitute, he went to Porte Dauphine three or four nights a week (including weekends), from 8:30 pm to around midnight.

of his mother's death: "Yes, I felt useless! Even though at that age, there's not much you can do...", and the fact that he "went through with it [prostituting himself]" gives the impression of "self-punishment". By prostituting himself, his image has "deteriorated[24]" - not least in his eyes - expressing the unease he felt at the time. In this situation, his motivation for prostitution was above all "destructive". For all that, prostitution enabled Julien - and still enables him - to give meaning to his life. In addition to the money it brings - thus offering a certain "comfort" in life - prostitution enables Julien to have a sexuality (he has no sexuality outside prostitution), to fill an emotional void, but also to "feel useful": "[...] And even I feel useful, I feel like I'm serving a purpose! - In relation to *what or to whom? -* Well, for the customers..."

Since the end of 2006[25], Julien has abandoned the sidewalk and now exclusively uses the Internet - deemed "less risky than the street" - to find customers. He doesn't have an advert or a blog, but logs on to "gay" dating sites to make new contacts: "So at first, I wanted to do a blog, that was in February... And then I gave up on that idea because I'm not very good at all that computer stuff! *(smiles)* And in fact I go to gay sites, like X dot com and stuff like that. Well, you have to be careful because you're not allowed to solicit, because there's a service, and if they see that you're soliciting for money or anything to do with money, you know, you can be banned from the site. And so I have to say all that on msn. So when someone arrives, I ask him if he has msn and all that, and he says yes, so he gives me his address, I give him mine and that's when I tell him that it's not free and that if he's interested, that's it. Although contact is established via the Internet, Julien's services and rates remain

---

24. Julien's first sexual experience was on the street, with a customer who "didn't even pay me". He has a bad memory of it and explains that "that's when I felt like a whore".

25. It was around this time that Julien signed up and began participating in the Forum.

identical to those he used to offer at Porte Dauphine. In fact, a number of the customers he met when he was a street hustler are still on his contact list today.

Since he's been hustling on the Web, and especially since he started taking part in Forum discussions, Julien has been questioning his practice - including his rates - and taking a "different look" at himself. He explains that forumers - escorts in particular - have made him "more aware of [his] body", and he's now trying to pay "more attention" to it. We understand here that the Forum - which is mainly used by occasional escorts, many of whom are students - embodies, in a way, a form of socialization into the practice of prostitution carried out by the latter. Indeed, the comments made on the Forum - by the escorts, but also by some of their customers - tend to soften "morals" and offer a more "acceptable" vision of prostitution. What's more, when we described the research field in the first part of this article, we saw that there were a number of rules on the Forum - particularly with regard to language - that had to be internalized. In this context, the discourse conveyed on the Forum by the escorts undoubtedly influenced Julien, who is now regaining self-esteem.

2.2.1 "I'm a prostitute, well, I'm an escort..."

In the prostitution arena, a distinction is made between the interviewees and other prostitutes in the names and terms used by the former - who prostitute themselves via the Internet - to describe their practice.

Like street prostitution, escorting falls under the generic term of "prostitution[26]". However, this prostitutional practice has created its own "jargon" to differentiate it from other forms of prostitution - particularly "traditional" prostitution. For example, on the Forum and during interviews, respondents do not speak of "prostitutes", but of "escorts" (or *escort girls*); the transaction is not described as a "pass", but rather as a "meeting" or "rendezvous"; as for the client, the name remains the same, except that in the discourse of escorts, he is often accompanied by positively connoted terms such as "charming", "courteous", "respectful", etc., which are often used to refer to the client.

Clearly, this vocabulary designates a particular service - marking a difference from that offered by "other" prostitutes - but the choice of terms is not insignificant. As the author of an article on Internet prostitution points out, "As soon as the term 'escort girl' is coined, the fantasy factory starts running at full speed. We imagine sumptuous creatures slipping into the arms of businessmen and Arab princes. Limousines, champagne, fine dining and fur coats[27]. While this imagery does not reflect the reality of all Net[28] prostitutes, the fact remains that escorting

---

26. Prostitution (from the Latin prostituere, "to put before", "to expose to the public") is an activity that consists of accepting or obtaining, in exchange for remuneration (or a promise of remuneration), sexual relations; Wikipedia, the Free Encyclopedia [07/23/2007], http://fr.wikipedia.org/wiki/Prostitution. A prostitute is therefore someone who "sells sexual services" in return for payment (usually money, but also material goods or services); MOSSUZ-LAVAU (Janine) and HANDMAN (Marie-Élisabeth), *La Prostitution à Paris*, Éditions de la Martinière, Paris, 2005, p. 11.

27. FRANCHON (Matthieu) and BITESNICH (Andreas), "Salariées le jour, escort girls la nuit", *Choc* (hebdomadaire), June 28 2007, no. 87, p. 29.

28. This imagery mainly concerns "VIP escorts" - see attached definition (Appendix 2).

refers - in the collective imagination at least - to the figure of the luxury prostitute. From this perspective, the use of words lends a less "vulgar" and more "enticing" character to the prostitutional act practiced by escorts, thus distinguishing them from other prostitutes, particularly "street prostitutes".

On the whole, students who prostitute themselves via the Internet use the jargon specific to escorting. They identify themselves as "escorts", and talk of "meetings" or "appointments" to describe their paid relationships. Some, however - like Anne-Sophie and Sandrine - aren't "afraid" of the words "prostitution" or "prostitute", but they always place it in a particular context: "Well, I'm an escort, so I prostitute myself, but uh... let's say it's prostitution but... non-professional! *(smiles)* I do it as a dilettante, you know! *(laughs)*" Similarly, in the discourse of student escorts, "the client isn't just a client." During her interview, Anne-Sophie - an occasional escort since November 2006 - insisted on using the term "man" rather than "client": "Client... I don't really like that word! What we're exchanging is a human relationship, not a commodity. [...] A customer is a human being, that's all!

In this context, we realize how important the use of words is. Not only do they serve to describe the activity of prostitution, they also reveal how the players view it, consider it and themselves. In Anne-Sophie's comment, we see that those involved in this form of prostitution see it as much more than just a paid sexual relationship.

2.2.2 A voluntary and free practice

According to Jean-Marc Philibert, a journalist with Le *Figaro*, "the vast majority of student prostitutes do everything in their power to avoid the street, where pimp networks are rife[29]."

> **"Knowing how to listen to your desires"**
>
> For Sandrine - an occasional escort since May 2006 - the fact of being a "free" prostitute greatly limits the "constraints" - by which she means the sometimes negative consequences of the activity - and appears to her to be essential for "living well as a prostitute".
>
> "The important thing for me is to have this desire. If tomorrow I don't feel like it, you see as I was saying, this summer I didn't feel like it, I really didn't feel like it, so I said no, I'm not dating, I can't do it! *(smiles)* And now it's the same... It's a bit of a whim! I'm letting myself go... But I find that in this area, it's better that I listen to myself... I really don't want to destroy myself psycho-logically so... [...] Yeah, I think that if you do it in a way... that you can be sick in the head, yeah sick in the head and sick in the skin, that you start to have very negative thoughts... For example, after a date to say to yourself: "you've been a whore"! I know that's what I said to myself after my first date! Now I can really see myself coming out of that hotel, and what's more, it was a shabby hotel! It was pouring with rain and I ran to my car... And there I was in my car and I burst into tears... It was really bad! And if one day it happened again like that, I'd stop right there and then, because... Well, I don't know how to explain it, because afterwards customer number 2 cheered me up and everything, but... But if I didn't feel well, I'd stop right there and then!..."
>
> This extract also shows that Sandrine is aware of the risks - particularly psychological - that prostitution entails, even when

---

29. PHILIBERT (Jean-Marc), "La prostitution gagne les bancs de la fac", *Le Figaro*, October 30, 2006, p. 11.

practiced occasionally. However, the knowledge that she can stop prostituting whenever she wishes gives her a "guarantee of security" and a certain sense of well-being in her approach to the act of prostitution.

This confirms OCRETH's statement[30] that student prostitution is more of an "independent activity". Consequently, students who choose to prostitute themselves do so without the constraint of a pimp, i.e. they carry out their prostitution according to their own requirements and on their own initiative. With no pimp, they are accountable to no one, and thus feel "*free*" of any "responsibility" or "constraint".

This autonomy enables them to organize their prostitution activities as they see fit, according to their "availability" and their "desires". Sandrine puts it this way: "I do it for me! I'm my own boss! [...] And I feel free, very free to do what I want, when I want... You see, there was a period when I was, I'm not going to say depressed, but I wasn't really in the mood and all, so I withdrew my ad. When I'd get messages, I'd say no, right now I don't feel like it... and that was that. I spent a month not meeting anyone. That was it."

The student escorts insist on the "freedom of action" they have in their prostitution practice. This freedom gives them the impression of being in control of their actions, and reinforces the impression of mastery and power they have over their own destiny.

---

30. OCRETH: Office central de la répression et de la traite des êtres humains.

2.2.3 Amateur, occasional and secondary prostitution

In contrast to the "professionals" for whom prostitution is their main activity (envisaged and practiced like any other profession), the prostitution practiced by students is secondary and allows them to "satisfy an occasional urge".

Students above all!

Students who prostitute themselves via the Internet emphasize their status as students. They devote most of their time to their studies, which remain their priority. As Annabelle - an occasional escort for nearly three years - puts it: "Well, I wasn't very available, so of course... Because I was really trying to give priority to my studies... Which meant that I couldn't necessarily meet people at any time". This unavailability, caused by their main activity, distinguishes them from "switchboard" professionals, i.e. those who do this, that you can call in an hour and hop, that's it! That's it, available all the time! Moreover, student escorts are sometimes somewhat condescending towards "always available" professionals. This illustrates the fact that they too belong to "another world", one where they are expected and recognized[31].

On the social scene, student escorts are known as students. It's true that their visibility as prostitutes is rather limited, especially compared to those who solicit on the street. What's more, most choose to keep this "parallel activity" a secret. The

---

31. In this regard, Becker points out that "most statuses - here that of prostitute - have a principal characteristic - here that of being a student - which serves to distinguish those who occupy this status from those who do not"; BECKER (Howard S.), *Outsiders - Études de sociologie de la déviance*, Éditions A.-M. Métailié, Paris, 1985, p. 55.

reasons for this "secrecy" - as varied and numerous as they are - underline the fact that, for these students, prostitution is not the activity that characterizes them. In this context, they relegate their prostitution to the background, regarding it more as "superfluous" or, in Sandrine's words, as an activity carried out "as a dilettante".

Time to spare

This secondary status is reflected in the way they manage their time, which is primarily devoted to their studies. In this context, student escorts fall into the "occasional[32]" category. Logically, this means that they don't seek to multiply the number of encounters or new partners. Quite often, their clientele is made up of a few "regulars" whom they see punctually from one month to the next. As well as ensuring a regular income, this practice saves them from "wasting precious time" looking for new customers, and also offers them a certain comfort since they already "know" these men. On this subject, Claire - an occasional escort since October 2006 - says that prostitution is "tiring, psychologically... Physically too, of course, but I mean psychologically, I mean it takes up a lot of time, it's... You see the time you spend thinking about it, making appointments, answering e-mails, all that is really invasive... I mean in your work, in your private life and so on. What made me try to stop, because when I couldn't do it, I was having trouble with my dates not working out and all that,

---

32. Occasional prostitutes - also known as "end-of-month prostitutes" - are people who occasionally exchange sex for money. This prostitutional practice is a "back-up activity" and brings together various profiles of people: students, people with a job or not...; NOR (Malika), *La Prostitution*, Éditions Le Cavalier Bleu, Paris, 2001, p. 54.

Student Prostitutes Online: In a Class All their Own?

well it just took up too much time, too much energy, you know... But now, it's because I'm just starting out and, you know, I don't necessarily know how to dress, and all that... It's also not easy to answer ads and know if it's someone serious, you know...". The fact of prostituting oneself at an unsteady pace takes on its full meaning, making the activity bearable: "I do it sporadically, once in a while... Whereas anyone else, well... I think it's all a question of rhythm. As soon as there's an accumulation, you..., you just can't! And then it's physiological, the body, it's not... As far as I'm concerned, my body says stop at some point! *(laughs)* It's not made for this all the time...". For these students, their bodies, and by extension themselves as people - body and mind combined - are not destined to be monetized "ten times a day". A future in which the intellectual function - embodied by the mind - takes precedence over the practical use of the body reduced to its sexual nature[33].

"I don't plan on doing this for the rest of my life!"

In addition to its occasional nature, the prostitution of our respondents is of a temporary nature. For the students, prostitution is seen as "a passing fancy" linked to a need and/or "a one-off desire". Indeed, all of them stress the temporary nature of the activity, and none of them see it as part of their future - a future which, as we have seen, will be of a completely different order. In

---

33. "The prostitution practiced by Iliana - a street prostitute - reduces everything. It reduces everything: the body to its function, the sexual act to its crude version, the person to an object. As we pass these girls, a strange reflex forbids us to compare. We decide they don't look like us. We identify these people with what they are at the moment we see them: the toys of a system"; DU-PONT-MONOD (Clara), *Histoire d'une prostituée*, Éditions Grasset & Fasquelle, Paris, 2003, p. 12.

fact, some of them plan to stop their venal encounters as soon as they no longer have or feel "the need" for them. Ambre - who has been an occasional prostitute since October 2005 - plans to "stop the activity once [her] debt has been repaid in full", and Claire is thinking of stopping paid relationships "as soon as [she's] done with them". On the other hand, the idea of "making a living out of it" in the long term is seen by the students as improbable, if not unacceptable. Sandrine, for example, says she "pities girls who tell themselves that it's the only way forward... because if [she] did it [prostitute herself] every day for a living, well... *(smile)* it wouldn't be the same!"

Once again, the student escorts demonstrate the limits of their prostitution practice. Their discourse highlights the fact that there are two quite distinct ways of prostituting oneself: an acceptable way - their own - and "that of the girls who make a living from it", considered "creepy" and "unbearable".

2.2.4 Internet solicitation

The means used by students to solicit contribute to this sense of security and freedom. Students who choose to prostitute themselves on an occasional basis generally solicit on the Web. To do so, they post ads on specialized sites - escort sites - or sometimes on classic dating sites[34]. Some also use chat rooms or discussion forums - as in the case of Anne-Sophie - or even have a personal blog.

As well as being easy to access and use, the Internet offers many advantages for student prostitutes. Firstly, it gives their

---

34. LARDELLIER (Pascal), *Le Cœur NET - Célibat et amour sur le Web*, Paris, Éditions Belin, 2004.

Student Prostitutes Online: In a Class All their Own?

advertisements a high profile, while preserving their anonymity. The Internet also offers the means to organize - from home - meetings with carefully selected clients. Finally, it remains - if we are to believe Julien's experience - a "less risky" practice than street soliciting.

Visibility and anonymity

Students are keen to keep their prostitution under wraps. The Internet appears to be the most effective means of doing so, as it offers the possibility of engaging in this practice while keeping their identity "intact". But in this kind of practice, remaining anonymous is a luxury. We know how stigmatized prostitution is[35] and we can easily imagine the consequences for the social and personal life of a student whose identity as a prostitute is revealed. On this subject, the student escorts are unanimous: it would be "impossible" for them to "live with the reputation of being a whore!", because as Anne-Sophie puts it, "it's too frowned upon in society, [...] people don't understand, they judge you, they break you... and you, you just have to, so you shut up!" By soliciting on the Net, the student runs a much lower risk of being recognized - and therefore of being subjected to the judgment of her peers - than if she worked directly on the street. What's more, student escorts use a variety of strategies to "cover their tracks". On their ads or personal blogs, they all use a pseudonym - their escort name - and avoid, as Claire does, "putting up photos of [their] face".

---

35. GOFFMAN (Erving), *Stigmate - Les usages sociaux des handicaps*, Les Éditions de Minuit, Paris, 1975.

The power of words

Many student escorts have their own blog. This tool, which is relatively simple to create, is - to use Sylvie Bigot's expression - "the escort's showcase[36]". Not only does this "shop window" enable the escort to present herself through a variety of photographs, but it also serves to spell out in detail her conditions and expectations with regard to paid relationships. In this context, "unlike their counterparts on the street [...] escorts have the power of words[37]". The students who prostitute themselves via the Internet can therefore, according to what they have written on their blog, hope to "attract" a clientele that meets, or at least accepts, their conditions. The texts on the blog explicitly frame - "it's written in black and white" - the conditions of the transaction (see box for an example).

Blog and *sine qua* non conditions

Here is an extract from Stéphanie's blog - student escort - which clearly illustrates the limits within which she conceives her prostitution practice:

- I travel exclusively to hotels for my meetings; I absolutely cannot receive guests at my home. This is a *non-negotiable* condition, and I do not go to your home for obvious security reasons. Ideally, I'd like to have a drink or dinner with you to get to know each other a little before considering a more intimate

---

36. BIGOT (Sylvie), *L'épanouissement sexuel des femmes au travers de l'escorting : mythe ou réalité ?* Journée regards insolites sur la sexualité - Regards artistiques et sociologiques sur la sexualité, Paris, École normale supérieure, June 2, 2007.

37. BIGOT (Sylvie), *ibid.*

meeting if you like me and if I feel comfortable and confident with you.

- I refuse to meet minors, of course, or men who are too young (under 25) for personal reasons, as well as people who seem discourteous or unpleasant for one reason or another.

- I don't make appointments for the same day or the next day, because that doesn't give us enough time to make sure we're compatible, and because my schedule doesn't allow it.

With this in mind, it's the escorts who choose their clients, not the other way round. Of course, it's the client who first initiates the process by contacting the escort likely to satisfy him. On the other hand, it's the escort who has the "last word", since it's she who decides whether or not to continue the relationship. In this case, the mechanisms of domination usually in place in this type of exchange are somewhat undermined[38]. Sandrine explains that, in her prostitution, she "doesn't sell [her] body", but "a right": "I allow this man to penetrate me, whereas under normal circumstances, he wouldn't be able to... well... You see, if he sees me in the street and wants to, well no, he can't! He's got to pay! And I have to accept! There's a kind of domination over them that... I don't know if it's really a domination, but it's a power that we exercise... They have no choice! *(smiles)*". To do this, student escorts set up a more or less lengthy "client selection" process. This selection is always carried out via the Net, through e-mail exchanges or msn conversations. This process can last several weeks, or even months for the most "reckless"

---

38. In the act of prostitution, "the buyer is the one who dominates: I have the power to buy another's body for my own well-being"; SCHAFF (Christelle), *op. cit.*, p. 27.

customers. This communication enables the student escorts to "get to know the personality" of the customer, "to see if a feeling is created", so as to retain only those who "correspond to [their] expectations". The buyer - the customer - is therefore not in the position of the one who disposes, but of the one whom the escort agrees or not to dispose of. However, this "choice to say no" is not often possible for street workers, and even less so for "pimped" prostitutes.

Less risky soliciting

When a person works as an independent prostitute - as is the case for a large majority of student escorts - one of the most serious risks is falling under the control of a pimp. In such a context, prostitution takes on an entirely different reality, where "physical and psychological violence become the daily lot of the pimp[39]". What's more, as Sélénia - a student who prostituted herself for over a year on the streets of Toulouse - testifies, "it's extremely difficult to get out of the pimp's clutches[40]". Although they do exist, the risks of being "spotted by a pimp" are much lower on the Internet than on the street.

The same applies to the authorities. Voluntary prostitution via the Internet seems to slip through the net of the police and tax authorities. As one lieutenant in a specialized department put it: "The activity of occasional workers is tolerated, and we turn a blind eye to this world[41].

---

39. LEGARDINIER (Claudine), *La Prostitution*, éditions Milan, Paris, 1996, p. 12.

40. Testimony of Sélénia in PHILIPPE (E.), "Étudiante, je me suis prostituée", *Esprit Femme* (mensuel), February 2007, no. 21, pp. 56-57.

41. FRANCHON (Matthieu), and BITESNICH (Andreas), *op. cit.*

Student Prostitutes Online: In a Class All their Own?

Finally, verbal and physical aggression from people - customers or passers-by - eager to "break the whore[42]" are logically less present in the reality of Net prostitutes[43]. The computer screen, while not all-powerful, lends a certain security to escorts, compared to what their street counterparts are exposed to. In fact, Julien's testimony - who prostituted himself on the street for over two years and now chooses to solicit on the Web - is quite explicit:

- Julien: "Well, firstly because the Internet is less risky, and secondly because there are cases, well I've seen cases... I've heard, for example, that now [...], the cops are more present and that in the Bois [de Boulogne] it's very risky now, so it's hot now!

- *Interviewer: Yes, and then with the Sarko laws, it...*

- Yes, with the laws! These laws have made things even worse for us! And it's not going to get any better because, for example, I know that Royal wants to penalize customers... So it's more difficult now, the customers, they might be more hesitant to stop because they can be arrested and then the passive soliciting and all that... [...] Whereas on the Internet, it's so, well you can't be punished by the law, all that... And then there are the assaults too! Well, I don't know about that, but with everything that's going on... you've got to be careful!

---

42. DUPONT-MONOD (Clara), *op. cit.* p. 55.

43. Escorts are not immune to being sent insulting, vulgar or even threatening messages. Some of them even tell stories of harassment (abundance of e-mails, repeated phone calls...) from anonymous or "rejected" customers, or even ex-customers.

On the other hand, as they prostitute themselves, student escorts are also more vulnerable[44]. In the event of a "bad encounter", no one is likely to come to their aid. That's why some have developed strategies to "secure" themselves. Ambre, for example, tells a friend - who is "open-minded" and lives nearby - every time she meets a customer. Not "lucky enough" to have "someone I can trust" to know about her paid relationships, Sandrine tells her clients that she has "a friend who [she] calls before and after [the meeting] to find out where [she is] and with whom..."

These precautions "relieve" them, but these students know that "it's a small price to pay" and that the risk of "running into a pervert" is present.

2.2.5 Making the pleasure last

As escorts, students who prostitute themselves via the Internet place the paid sexual relationship within a relationship that goes beyond strictly sexual interaction. This is why they prefer "long encounters", which give them the time to "get to know each other better" and create the illusion of a more "natural" meeting, where money becomes a "formality". As a result, escort prostitution is not the same as a 15-minute pass with a street prostitute[45].

In escorting, appointments last a minimum of one hour, and can be extended for an evening, a weekend or even several

---

44. PHILIPPE (E.) and ADJOVI (L.), "Malaise dans l'université : étudiantes le jour, prostituées la nuit", *Jasmin* (hebdomadaire), November 27, 2006, no. 6, p. 12.
45. BIGOT (Sylvie), *op. cit.*

Student Prostitutes Online: In a Class All their Own?

days. Escort rates are set according to the length of the meeting - hourly rates - and not "per service" as Julien puts it: "I don't count the hours, but I work on a per-service basis... In the meantime, it usually lasts 30-45 minutes. Well, there are the faster ones too! *(smiles)* and this one lasts 10-15 minutes! So yes, it's not the same, it's shorter than escorts... And so, you see, I charge 50 euros for a blowjob and 75 for sex... In fact, I charge the usual rates. Of course, when I go on the Forum and see escorts asking 200 or 300 euros an hour, I'm... I'm completely out of step! But anyway, we're not doing the same thing, the service is different."

Similarly, while Julien - like street prostitutes - is paid for a specific sexual practice (and the choice is limited), student escorts offer a more or less exhaustive range of practices, which they bundle into an hourly "package". As a result, the sexual act is less "mechanical" and seems much closer to "making love" than to the simple exchange of "courtesies" practiced in traditional[46] practice. Of course, to achieve this "ideal" vision of paid sex, escorts need to feel sufficiently confident with their customers. From this perspective, rigorous customer selection makes sense.

"We don't just have sex! We talk a lot too..."

For a venal rendezvous to meet the expectations of student escorts, it must include time, of varying length, given over to "discussions, exchanges... other things!" The latter insist that their prostitution practice "isn't just about that! [to sex]", and emphasize what they refer to as *social time*. In the prostitutional

---

46. SCHAFF (Christelle), *op. cit.* p. 51.

relationship, *social time* corresponds to the moment(s) other than the one(s) during which the actual sexual act takes place. It therefore refers to the various times of exchange - in terms of communication - between the client and the prostitute[47]. As Sandrine explains: "And in fact, beyond sex, there are also, well, humanly speaking, there are a lot of things. Some of them really surprise me, because they [the customers] are really interested in you! We talk a lot, we exchange a lot, I mean, I have the impression that they consider me a person in my own right..."

Beyond the pleasures of "exchanging" and "getting to know someone", *social time* serves above all to "humanize" the act of prostitution. In this context, the student escort does not feel reduced to "an object to be consumed[48]". On the contrary, she feels considered, in Sandrine's words, "as a person in her own right". Consideration and respect for the Other - in this case, the escort - are two aspects that shine through in the discourse of students who prostitute themselves via the Internet. Many of them admit that these encounters enhance their self-esteem, as they are recognized - by the customer - "at [their] fair value": "The fact that we have this exchange, this reciprocity... I mean, it's not fair... The guy who comes to see me, he doesn't just come to get laid! *(smiles)* Otherwise he'd choose a more professional girl, a bit cheaper *(smiles)* and that's that! What's more, he wouldn't spend three hours with me, whereas you

---

47. This type of communication seems to be absent (or almost absent) in Julien's prostitution:- Julien: "So I've never been to a restaurant with a customer, I've never accompanied a customer anywhere, it's just the sex act, they just pay me for the sex act.- *Interviewer: Ok. Because you know, it's when the girls, they talk about* social time...

48. Dupont-Monod (Clara), *op. cit.* p. 12.

can do that in fifteen minutes! *(laughs)*" This respectful atmosphere underlines the mutual interest expected by the student escort and the customer. The escort expects her customer to be interested in her - as a person - before her body. The customer, on the other hand, expects the escort to be interested in him - as a person - before his money. In this type of relationship, it's sincerity that's most important. In this respect, Bertrand - a chartered accountant, married for some twenty years and a regular customer of student escorts - explains that, for him, the relationships he has with "his escorts" are not "impersonal", it's not: we arrive, jump on each other and leave! It's not like that at all!... It has to be a meeting, or at least an exchange that's meant to be, well, a human relationship after all! One that includes sex, but also something else!... What I'm waiting for is a real encounter! [...] A truly successful encounter is somewhere beyond the purchase! Well, the money's there, it's there, but... Well, you don't think about it anymore!

This *social time* gives a "natural" character to a contractual, framed meeting. In fact, many student escorts call themselves "GFE[49]", meaning that they try, not least in their attitude, to make the venal encounter "happen naturally", as if they were the "official" of the clients. In this case, student escorts present themselves as they are in "real life", without artifice or "pretense". Anne-Sophie, for example, explains that she "doesn't change a thing" about herself: "I am just the way I am! Sometimes, when I come back from the pool, I arrive with my hair wet and my sports bag on my arm... Well, that's just the way it is! If they like

---

49. *Girl-friend experience.* This term is part of the escorting jargon; see Appendix 2 for further details on the definition of "GFE".

me, fine, if not, too bad! Through this "natural" behavior, student escorts mark their difference from other prostitutes - the professionals - who "aren't themselves, who pretend to be, who are elsewhere...". They assert the authenticity of their way of being, doing and conceiving "human relationships".

The "GFE" experience implies that both the escort and the customer invest themselves personally and sincerely in the relationship. In this way, both parties reveal themselves and agree to "drop the mask". During the appointment, the protagonists exchange views on a variety of subjects, "even the most personal". For the student escorts, these exchanges are "privileged" moments, as they offer them the opportunity to discover "a little more fragility in people [customers] who a priori have nothing fragile about them". In this context, the figure of the "all-powerful" customer is called into question, because by revealing themselves, they expose their weaknesses. In this respect, Sandrine feels she "knows" her "regulars" well, "maybe even better than their own wives".

Last but not least, the term "GFE" also applies to the sexual act itself. Many student escorts say they "have fun" during sex. In addition, tenderness, caresses, foreplay and even "kisses"[50] are just some of the attentions that help to make the act of sexual intercourse "natural". As far as money is concerned, it can be temporarily "forgotten" or "forgotten", if the relationship proves to be "really sincere". This does not mean that sex becomes free, but rather that the escort's attitude towards the customer, and vice versa, erases the framework within which

---

50. In the traditional prostitutional relationship, prostitutes don't kiss their clients or let their hair or face be stroked. André Téchiné's 1991 film *J'embrasse pas* highlights this reality.

Student Prostitutes Online: In a Class All their Own?

the encounter takes place. Many student escorts talk about the "discomfort" they sometimes feel at receiving money in return for their services. Yet we know that money is the central element in the act of prostitution, since it seals the relationship and makes it possible. And yet, for these escorts, who behave towards their customers in much the same way - or almost the same way - as they do towards their "free" lovers, the boundaries between "free" and "paying" relationships can sometimes become blurred, resulting in a feeling of "non-legitimacy in getting paid".

2.2.6 Special customers

Student escorts have a very specific customer profile. In addition to the fact that many of them are "mature" men - aged between 40 and 55 - mostly married and with "a good professional situation", their expectations of a venal relationship echo those of student escorts. They're looking for "ordinary, natural girls" to share a moment of "the pleasure of the flesh", but also - and this shouldn't be forgotten - "the pleasure of being together".

Most of these men were once customers of "professional" street prostitutes. However, as Michel - a bank consultant who has been married for some twenty years and is now a client of occasional escorts, some of them students - points out, these encounters often ended in "a certain frustration". For these men, classic passes are "too poor erotically", but also - and they insist on this point - "not rich enough from a human point of view". That's why today, they prefer paid encounters with occasional escorts, encounters that seem to satisfy them in every way.

Like student escorts, these customers prefer "ongoing relationships" in which they can develop a "deep bond", even "friendship", between themselves and "venal girls". As a result, many choose to meet a limited number of escorts, but prefer regular appointments. In this context, the escort is a kind of "mistress", since the relationship is regular and ongoing. However, the approach is less risky, as there is normally no romantic feeling (and therefore no commitment) on the part of either the client or the escort. Money is also used to settle accounts after each encounter. By becoming their "regulars", customers enter into a "privileged relationship" with the student escorts, or - in Bertrand's words - a "lover-lover relationship filled with friendship". In this regard, Ambre mentions that her "four regulars have become friends". She points out that she can check up on them "just like that, for free" between appointments. We can assume that this process is a way of building customer loyalty... Nevertheless, the approach seems sincere.

The pleasure of the Other...

Clients of student escorts also attach importance to the fact that "the girl is doing it [prostituting herself] for pleasure too". This is why they refuse to meet "a pimped-up girl", because, as Bertrand explains: "I don't feel comfortable endorsing this kind of thing". In their discourse, customers emphasize a certain "ethic" and defend the fact that there is such a thing as "free prostitution, freely consented to", where the prostitute's pleasure is not feigned. According to them, their own pleasure is also "the escort's pleasure". This allows them to feel valued, as they are able to "give pleasure to a woman". This mark of attention is also mentioned by several student escorts, such as Claire - who to date has met four clients: "Frankly, the ones I've met have been super charming, pleasant and have known a lot of women, so in sexual terms, they're good lovers... Well, maybe they're not all like that, but the ones I've selected in any case... I mean, I don't feel like I've come across any losers! In this context, and this ties in with what we saw earlier, this prostitutional practice is closer to a paid "lover-mistress" relationship than to a traditional pass.

In this section, we've seen that - in certain respects - the prostitution practiced by student escorts falls into a different register from that practiced by traditional professional prostitutes. Moreover, traditional prostitutes and student escorts do not have the same expectations of the activity. While for the former, prostitution is seen as a "profession" enabling them to earn money, the latter don't imagine that they can "make a living" in a sustainable way by prostituting themselves. Their prostitution is only envisaged according to strict, personalized rules - i.e., in line with their desires - and on a short-term basis. Moreover, they see their prostitution as a form of paid "libertinage". In this context, students who prostitute themselves along the lines of occasional escorts are prostitutes in a league of their own, both in form and in the way they represent prostitution. It is precisely this particularity that distinguishes student escorts from traditional professional prostitutes, as the form and nature of their prostitution is more akin to that of "luxury prostitution".

Yet there's one common characteristic that brings student escorts closer to other prostitutes. All of them have experienced - or are experiencing - a number of ruptures in their life trajectory. We'll look at this in the next section.

Part Three: Breakdowns

The prostitution of student escorts is a response to various significant ruptures in their life histories. Although they all prostitute in a similar way, the reasons and motivations that led them to make this choice are different. For some, prostitution is first and foremost a "utilitarian" goal - to earn money - in order to continue their studies. For some, it embodies a kind of "forbidden fantasy" enabling them to break with traditional family values. For others, it's more a question of "revenge" on the men with whom they've had gratuitous relationships. From these diverse realities, we can identify three patterns of breakdown: social and financial breakdowns, breakdowns in relation to family morality, and breakdowns in relation to gratuitous love relationships.

But these patterns are not set in stone, and some students combine different, self-perpetuating breaks.

3.1 READY FOR ANYTHING TO SUCCEED

To finance their studies, pay the rent or make ends meet, some students choose to prostitute themselves. While figures on the scale of the phenomenon are uncertain - "to date, there are no serious scientific studies on the subject[1]" - one of the causes leading to this practice is certainly linked to the impoverishment of students. In this regard, Guillaume Houzel - Chairman of the Observatoire de la Vie Etudiante (OVE) - declares: "For several years now, we have been witnessing increasing pressure on students' purchasing power. With the rise in property prices, their housing expenses are increasing... but not the amount of their grants[2]". According to the Dauriac report[3] on the economic precariousness of students, 100,000 students in higher education are living below the poverty line, set at around 650 euros per month per person. According to the OVE, more than 45,000 students are currently living in extreme poverty, and 225,000 are struggling to finance their studies[4].

1. Remarks by the spokeswoman for the SUD-Étudiant union whom I interviewed in Paris on January 19, 2007.

2. PHILIBERT (Jean-Marc), *op. cit.*

3. Jean-François Dauriac was successively Director of the CROUS in the Créteil academy (from 1992 to 2001), then in the Versailles academy (until 2004). In 2000, Claude Allègre - then Minister of Education - asked Jean-François Dauriac to draw up a report on the economic situation of students in France, with a view to implementing a "Student Social Plan". DAURIAC (Jean-François), *Note de synthèse du Rapport au ministre de l'Éducation nationale de la Recherche et de la Technologie sur la mise en œuvre du plan social étudiant*, Paris, 2000.

4. PHILIBERT (Jean-Marc), *op. cit.* ; There are 2,200,000 students in France today.

It should be remembered that this impoverishment affects a certain category of students, namely those whose parents are unwilling or unable to support them financially, and who consequently have to fend for themselves - or nearly so - to meet their needs and continue their studies.

3.1.1 *Social and financial shortcomings*

In their current lives as students, working- and middle-class women experience a number of social and financial shortcomings that compromise - to a greater or lesser extent - their pursuit of higher education. As we have already seen, academic success is of paramount importance to these students. In addition to personal gratification, pursuing higher education offers them the opportunity to establish their ambition - to "make something of themselves" - and to secure a more "comfortable" lifestyle than the one they experienced in their families. However, neither these students nor their families have the financial resources to fully realize this ambition. Sandrine's story is an apt illustration of this reality. In particular, it shows the situation in which this student finds herself, and reveals the alternatives Sandrine has opted for to be able to "pursue [her] dreams" and one day become an "architect".

It was on the advice of a Forum customer - who had commented several times on my topic - that I contacted Sandrine. Before agreeing on a date and place for our meeting, we communicate at length by e-mail and mp. This is my first interview with a student escort, so I take care to detail the approach and purpose of the survey in order to "reduce as much as possible the interviewee's reluctance to provide information to a stranger whose exact use she doesn't know[5]".

As agreed, we meet in downtown Lille, just after Sandrine's class. She presents an image of a "classic" student. She's wearing a dark turtleneck sweater, dark pants and a black coat. She's wearing no make-up and her hair is tied back. While we look for a "suitable" place for the interview, we talk for about twenty minutes about our studies, our projects and so on. This time allows each of us to get to know the other better, and establishes a certain climate of trust. Once we're settled in a rather quiet tea room, I go into more detail about my research. Sandrine seems tense, but is obviously keen to talk about her experience. Before formally beginning the interview, she points out that she can sometimes be "incoherent" and that her speech can be "paradoxical". She fears that I won't "understand" her. Indeed, at the start of the interview, Sandrine remains "reserved". Her body is set back from the table, she speaks quite low, her answers are brief and punctuated by a little "embarrassed" laughter. When we broach the subject of prostitution, however, she becomes more at ease and offers detailed answers. After the interview, we continue to communicate by e-mail and meet up again three months later for an informal get-together with Claire, another student escort and Forum participant. This meeting sheds some light on Sandrine's career path.

<hr>

5. PINSON (Michel) and PINSON-CHARLOT (Monique), *Voyage en grande bourgeoisie - Journal d'enquête*, PUF, Paris, 2005 (2nd updated edition - 1st ed.: 1997), pp. 34-35.

Limited financial resources

Sandrine is 22 years old and currently in her third year of architecture school. After obtaining her baccalauréat, she left her family home and native region to enter a preparatory class and then enter a grande école in Lille. Despite living "over 500 kilometers away", Sandrine's parents visit her regularly, "about one weekend every month and a half". They are present "at [her] side" and give her moral support, but they are unable to provide financially for her needs. And yet, a student's purchasing power - and by extension his or her living conditions - is closely linked to that of his or her parents, since family support is generally the primary source of income for students[6]. Sandrine's parents "don't have much money", and are currently in a "difficult financial situation". Her father - an ex-retailer - has been unemployed for six years, and her mother - a nursery assistant - "doesn't earn much". What's more, they are "already" supporting her older sister - four years her senior - who "still lives with them" and, after a long illness, is starting a new training course. In this context, Sandrine is "embarrassed" to be a burden on her parents, and doesn't want to ask them for more money. She explains that "they [her parents] don't have to take responsibility for [her] choices", which is why she prefers "not to ask them for anything", because in her opinion, "they already have enough of a ball and chain [her sister] at home". In a way, Sandrine is aware of the investment "her" choices represent. Having opted for a Grande École education with relatively high

---

6. Assistance from parents and other family members accounts for nearly 44.6% of students' resources [CREDOC figure - 1992]; GALLAND (Olivier) and OBERTI (Marco), *op. cit.* p. 67.

tuition fees - compared to a public university in particular - and, what's more, in a city other than the one where her family lives, Sandrine knows - given her family's resources - that her choices entail a certain number of sacrifices. In this respect, she points out that her parents are "a little out of touch" with the current cost of living: "my parents, with 200 euros a month, they think we live well! Despite this realization, Sandrine doesn't want to give up on her dreams, and - so as not to involve her parents - wants to "manage on my own and get there on my own". What's more, living in her own home gives her greater autonomy when it comes to organizing her life.

Many authors[7] agree that students are not equal when it comes to financing their studies, and that the advantages - particularly economic - enjoyed by young people from wealthy backgrounds, but lacking by those from less privileged backgrounds, result in unequal access to higher education. The French government, aware of this "inequality of opportunity", has set up a system to provide financial assistance to certain young people (scholarships based on social criteria, merit-based scholarships, housing allowances, etc.), thus offering them a "fundamental tool for the social elevator[8]". However,

---

7. Examples include BOURDIEU (Pierre), *Les Héritiers, op. cit*; BOUDON (Raymond), *L'Inégalité des chances, op. cit*; DUBET (François), "Les étudiants", in DUBET (F.) *et al, Universités et villes*, L'Harmattan, Paris, 1994; BEAUD (Stéphane), *80 % au bac... et après? op. cit*; EURIAT (M.) and THELOT (C.), "Le recrutement social de l'élite scolaire en France", *Revue française de sociologie*, XXXVI-3, July-September 1995, pp. 403-438.

8. In 2006, student aid amounted to 6 billion euros, benefiting 2.2 million students. Source: WAUQUIEZ (Laurent), *Les aides aux étudiants : comment relancer l'ascenseur social*, Paris, 2006.

this system is obviously not without its faults, and only partially covers students' needs. Over the past five years, compulsory expenses - registration fees, social security, accommodation, university restaurant meals, etc. - have risen by 23%, while university grants and housing allowances have increased by only 10%[9].

Sandrine, who has been on a scholarship since the start of her higher education studies, feels that state aid is no more than a "top-up". Indeed, she expresses the limited effect that this type of scheme has on her own situation: "Yes, I have the grants and let's just say that I oscillated and still oscillate between echelon 0 and echelon 1 of the grant. The problem with level 0 is that you don't get anything at all, and if you're on level 1, you don't get much... Let's just say it's not bad, it does help a little with tuition fees... [...] Level 1 is 1,200 euros for the year, yeah 1,200 euros a year. So if you count that per month, well... That's barely 100 euros per month, even less... [...] with scholarships, it's not enough. The State and the others [her classmates] don't realize! Sandrine's final comment under-lines the fact that, despite state aid, the inequalities between her and her classmates - most of whom come from privileged social backgrounds - persist. In this respect, she adds that few of her classmates "manage without mom and dad", and that in this context, they are "less aware of realities", particularly with regard to money and the cost of living in general. Sandrine feels that she is "more deserving" than her fellow students to succeed in her studies, as she has to "work twice as hard". Indeed, as she

---

9. PHILIBERT (Jean-Marc), *op. cit.*

has to finance her own studies[10], it is imperative for her to have a paid job alongside her studies.

Balancing study and paid work

In 2003, 45.5% of French students were gainfully employed during the academic year (excluding summer vacations)[11]. Since becoming a student, Sandrine - like 26.6% of students who work alongside their studies[12] - has occasionally looked after children. During her second year at architecture school, she looked after a young child for six months, three nights a week[13]. For Sandrine, this work was "a godsend", as it was difficult to find a job that fitted in with her studies: "[...] I had to find a little job and all that... In the beginning, I did quite a lot of baby-sitting actually. [...] In fact, what happened last year was... I found a... I really wanted to try and earn as much as I could, because with my studies, my hours are pretty... shitty *(laughs)* as you can see! They change all the time, so I can't work in a store or for a real boss. I looked in the

---

10. It's worth remembering, however, that for Sandrine, self-financing is also a personal choice. Although her parents are in a difficult financial situation, it is she who chooses "not to ask them for anything", and thus to be autonomous. This autonomy, as we have seen, is reinforced by the fact that she owns her own home, and also underlines her desire to emancipate herself from her family, to be master of her own life and choices.

11. GRIGNON (Claude) (chairman of the OVE scientific committee), *Les étudiants en difficulté : Pauvreté et précarité - Rapport au Ministre de la Jeunesse*, de l'Éducation nationale et de la Recherche, Paris, 2003.

12. GRIGNON (Claude), *ibid.* - The paid activities of students unrelated to their studies are very diverse: the most frequent are babysitting (26.6%), commercial "jobs" (20.2%) and private lessons (16.7%).

13. It was on this occasion that she became aware of the existence of *escort girls*. The mother of the child she was looking after "was a hostess in a cork bar in Lille" and "sometimes met people as an escort". She regularly talked to Sandrine about her experiences.

classified ads, at the CROUS... but there was never anything for me! I mean, I was never available because of my classes! But this job was a godsend! Thanks to her babysitting, Sandrine earned 300 euros a month, enabling her "not to depend too much on [her] parents". On the other hand, Sandrine feels that having this job has handicapped her in carrying out her studies properly: "But on the other hand it showed in the second semester, I missed all my midterms except one!" This reality echoes the work carried out by the Observatoire de la vie étudiante (Student Life Observatory), which points out that holding a paid job while studying increases "the risk of failure or dropping out[14]". These risks arise from the competition - particularly in terms of time - between the "student job" and the demands of university work. According to the OVE, this is the context in which the notion of student job insecurity should be understood.

Given the somewhat mixed results of her second semester, Sandrine realizes that "she's going to have to find something else [another paid job]" to support herself and maintain her independence from her parents, without jeopardizing her academic success.

3.1.2 Prostitution as a support for social shortcomings

In May 2006, Sandrine began to find out more about the escorting business. The mother of the child she was baby-sitting had already spoken to her several times about her "hostess" and escorting activities. At the time, Sandrine didn't "[see herself] as

---

14. GRIGNON (Claude), *op. cit.*

an escort", as she didn't "really have the head for it[15]!" However,
after giving up babysitting, Sandrine began researching on the
Web and discovered "lots of girls [escort girls]" with whom she
could identify. Driven by "curiosity" and the need for money,
Sandrine placed an ad on an online escort girl website. To her
astonishment, she soon received her first solicitations from
customers.

Sandrine began prostituting herself at the end of May 2006.
Today, she meets two or three clients a month - mainly regulars - and earns between 400 and 600 euros a month. According
to her, occasional escorting has the advantage of "earning a lot
of money quickly", saving her "the hassle of going to work for a
month to earn the same... or even less[16]!"

The power of money

When Sandrine began working as a prostitute, the money
she earned from her sexual encounters was mainly used "to
replenish the accounts, pay the rent, whatever was a bit urgent
at the time! In this context, she sees her prostitution as an urgent
need for money. In fact, she had gone into debt with friends and
was "a month behind with the rent! Today, although Sandrine is
no longer in an emergency situation, she continues to prostitute
herself to meet her daily needs and remain "totally independent
of [her] parents".

---

15. Before becoming a prostitute, Sandrine imagined escorts as being "beautiful women, tall, slim, blonde... models, in fact", i.e. a far cry from the profile of
the "ordinary girl", which she understands to be her own.

16. As an example, I worked for 6 months - in parallel with my studies - in a
shop for 25 hours a week. My salary was 715.25 euros.

We understand that prostitution enables student escorts like Sandrine to pursue their studies under favorable material conditions - daily needs such as rent and food are covered - while leaving them enough time to work on their courses and hope to pass their university year. Similarly, Sandrine's escorting business is flexible to her "ever-changing" schedule, enabling her to adapt the number of clients "according to [her] needs". On this subject, she points out that she now uses part of the money she earns from her prostitution to "indulge herself". Before becoming an escort, Sandrine felt she "didn't enjoy herself enough". With her limited budget, she rarely went out, thus setting herself further apart from her classmates "who go out super often". In a way, money allows her to integrate into this group of students - for whom money, it should be remembered, is not a real concern - and to socialize with their practices. In fact, now that she "has the means", Sandrine is more willing to take part in the activities proposed by her colleagues: "well, now when they have a restaurant, I go too!"

Describing herself as "not at all a spendthrift", Sandrine saves part of her prostitution money in order to anticipate possible changes in her life and guarantee, "at least until the end of [her] studies", her current "comfortable" lifestyle. With this in mind, Sandrine schedules more fee-based appointments than she actually needs to support her current lifestyle, with the aim of "putting money aside... just in case!" This strategy enables her to take a calmer view of her future, which, without this money, could be in jeopardy. She feels that, with her savings, she will have sufficient resources to continue and complete her studies. What's more, she explains that "if one day [she no longer has] the desire [to prostitute] or [if] tomorrow [she] falls in love[17]", she will be able to count - for a while at any rate - on her savings. From her words, we can see that prostitution is not a long-term prospect, and that her future career as an architect remains her primary objective.

Customer socialization

Because of the specific nature of their prostitution, student escorts have a particular type of customer. With some of them - their "regulars" in particular - they develop almost friendly relationships, in which both parties are involved in more than just a sexual relationship. Their customers are mainly mature men from relatively favorable professional and economic backgrounds. Most of them belong to the ruling classes.

Respectful, respectable customers

Sandrine confides that she "gets on well with her customers" and that some of them could even be "boyfriends". With one of them, she spent four "magnificent" days abroad "in a superb luxury hotel". She says they dined in a restaurant and "discussed lots of things [...] like a couple!" Her customers seem to behave like perfect "gentlemen". They know and practice gallantry, and regularly demonstrate courtesy: "You see, they [her customers] speak well, well they listen to you, they don't cut you off [...]."

---

17. For Sandrine, escorting is incompatible with a romantic relationship. In fact, fidelity within a couple is a value to which she adheres and, above all, to which she aspires for her future life as a woman and wife.

His clientele is made up mainly of well-to-do men: "Yeah, honestly yeah... they're rather... I'm not going to lie... Because to be able to pay 600 euros every three months, well that's okay! What's more, you have to be able to afford it without your wife noticing, and that can't be easy... And so my most regular, the one I see every month, he's the head of a company, a big company and... well, there's no problem for him! And the one I used to see a lot but decided to stop seeing, he was also a company director, but next door he had a company in which he owned all the shares... So that gives you an idea! *(laughs)* Well, I've met a few more modest ones, but that's not the rule! And then, I've often met them for an hour... Well, I don't really like hour-long meetings because I can't keep to an hour! Because I need to talk, I need to get to know each other, I need to feel good and all that...". In this context, the customers Sandrine meets are not like the men she used to rub shoulders with in her family or even in her life in general. They belong to "another world" - different from her own, by the way - which she learns to know and appreciate.

Some of Sandrine's customers have offered to help her if she ever needs it: "By the way, he [a regular customer] is one of the people [customers] who have left me their contact details if I ever have a problem... They're ready to use their, even their profession, well their situation to help out... So there you go, after him I said to myself ah bah sometimes that's really good! *(smiles)* And there you go! This approach underlines the fact that, through her prostitution, Sandrine has built up a "network" whose influence on the social scene is not negligible. As a result, she makes up - thanks to the capital owned by her customers - for a handicap inherited from her original social background. Her customers help to increase her social capital[18].

Mentors

For student escorts who prostitute themselves in the same way as Sandrine, customers are often presented as men who "understand" them, i.e. people with whom they share a certain number of values and practices. In addition to sharing a certain freedom of sexual mores, clients - not least because of their profession - possess knowledge and experience that the escorts like to learn from. In this respect, Claire - a student escort whose background is similar to Sandrine's - talks about her clients as being people with "good jobs, often engineers by the way, who could be from my school and with whom I can chat, given that I move in the same milieu, so to speak... [...] Intellectually and sexually, it's very interesting [to be in the company of this type of person]. Intellectually, because these are people who have lived more, who have perspective, who have a good situation, conversation...". From this interview extract, we understand that student escorts don't just see their clients as people who "receive" - in this case a sexual service in exchange for money - but also as people who "bring" them, intellectually and culturally in particular. In this context, the men the students

---

18. In addition to their *habitus* - which refers to the set of more or less unconscious, lasting dispositions acquired within the social milieu of origin and which guide the perceptions, opinions and actions of individuals - *social classes* are characterized, according to Bourdieu, by the volume of economic (material wealth), cultural (intellectual knowledge, diplomas, etc.) and social (social relations, networks of acquaintances) capital they can mobilize in their social interactions. Thus, the classes at the top of the social hierarchy bring together the most capital-rich individuals.

meet in the context of venal relations pass on a certain amount of knowledge to them, knowledge that is valued on the social scene. Bertrand's comments - a client of occasional escorts, some of whom are also students - are quite revealing in this respect: "Yes, we [he and the escorts] share um... It's a sharing of the pleasure of being together, not automatically physical pleasure I'll say, but the pleasure of being together, that... Well, an encounter with an escort, I'll say it's not, it's not... well mainly sex, but it's not only sex! I mean, that's why you go to an escort, that's for sure! But a lot of people will tell you that... and I think it's clear from the people who do, well from this category of people I'll say, there's what's called *social time (smile)*... And so it's this *social time* that makes it go, well there's a certain feeling that's created, we discuss something else,... Well, with one of my last meetings, we ended up talking about Beethov' 9th *(smile)*... And that the person didn't know anything about it, and the next day, he bought Beethov' 9th! *(laughs)*" In a way, customers socialize student escorts to the codes in force in privileged social circles[19], circles to which they are destined thanks to their studies and intended profession.

Similarly, female students like Sandrine and Claire sometimes receive relevant advice on their training from this type of man - some of our customers have followed the same academic path. They can also talk to them about their studies and career aspirations, without feeling "out of step". This feeling of being "out of step" is particularly acute when they discuss these subjects with their families, especially their parents, who don't always understand their choices. On this subject, Vincent de

---

19. BOURDIEU (Pierre), *La Distinction - Critique sociale du jugement, op. cit.*

Gaulejac explains that "changes in class [background] pose particularly visible problems between children in high promotion and their parents[20]". We've seen that upwardly mobile female students - such as Sandrine and Claire - are driven to use a different language, acquire a different *habitus*, and integrate a different world, provoking "a cognitive, existential and social dissonance" in their relations with their elders. In this context, Vincent de Gaulejac points out that social distance, "whether in the form of progressive estrangement or not, reactivates ambivalence, provokes misunderstandings and fuels guilt on both sides[21]". This is why - like Sandrine - student escorts aspire to a certain independence from their families, marking their difference from their own.

3.2. BREAKING OUT OF "SHACKLES"

Today, even if sexuality is not "free", since - like all social interaction - it is embedded in a certain number of relationships (gender, class, generation, cultural...), it is perceived as being, *a priori,* less and less codified[22]. In this regard, Michel Bozon points out that one of the major changes in generational relations between the 1960s and the 2000s is that "the parents' generation has given up setting restrictive standards for young

---

20. GAULEJAC (Vincent DE), *La Névrose de classe - Trajectoire sociale et conflit d'identité*, Hommes & Groupes Éditeurs, Paris, 1987, p. 84.
21. GAULEJAC (Vincent DE), *ibid.*
22. LAQUEUR (Thomas), *La Fabrique du sexe - Essai sur le corps et le genre en Occident,* Éditions Gallimard, Paris, 1992.

120

people[23]. The possibility of experiencing "real youth" has gradually become widespread, and their "private autonomy" is generally accepted. In this context, parents no longer condemn their children's active love lives - which can sometimes even take place under their own roof. Of course, this does not apply to all contemporary families. Some, like Anne-Sophie's and Annabelle's, retain traditional values and exert greater control over their children's sexuality. For these students, prostitution is not about the need for money, but rather about breaking with traditional family values and satisfying "a forbidden fantasy".

3.2.1 Breaking with family values

Student escorts at odds with family morality are students raised in families where traditional values - linked to religious morality - embody the family norm. In these conservative families, young people's entry into sexuality takes place under the watchful eye and control of relatives (and possibly elders). Parents set the rules by which their children - especially girls - can access this statutory activity of maturity[24]. In this context, children's dating and outings - especially in adolescence - are often tightly controlled by parents. Similarly, the topic of sexuality remains somewhat taboo and is rarely brought to the fore in family discussions. Anne-Sophie's story illustrates this reality.

---

23. Parents do, however, keep a watchful eye on their children's sexual practices, particularly with regard to the risks of sexually transmitted infections or unplanned pregnancy; BOZON (Michel), *Sociologie de la sexualité*, Armand Colin, 2005, p. 54.

24. BOZON (Michel) *ibid*, p. 16.

It was on the recommendation of a Forum customer - with whom I'd spoken on several occasions - that Anne-Sophie suggested I be interviewed. We exchanged a few Mp's and quickly agreed on a date to meet. We meet after class at the exit of a metro station, not far from her university. As she walks towards me, Anne-Sophie introduces herself as a rather reserved young woman who seems a little unsure of herself. She looks like a "high-school girl": rather short, slim and dressed in jeans, she's wearing sneakers and carrying a backpack. Her hair is loose, and she has no jewelry or make-up. Before the interview begins, she politely declines to be recorded, as she is "not too comfortable talking about this[25]". During the course of the interview, and depending on the topics discussed, Anne-Sophie appears more or less "at ease", touched, angry... When we broach the subject of family and relations with her parents, Anne-Sophie has tears in her eyes (she actually cries twice), and uses a scornful, ironic tone when referring to her parents (mainly her mother).

A traditional education

Anne-Sophie is 21, an only child and lives with her parents, both of whom are nearing the end of their professional careers. Her parents - office workers - are nearly 40 years apart from their daughter. This age gap is practically the equivalent of two generations, and underlies the misunderstandings that can exist between a young student just starting out in her adult life, and adults who are now coming to the end of their professional lives.

---

25. During the interview, however, Anne-Sophie gave me permission to take notes, and to transcribe some of what she said.

For Anne-Sophie, her parents are "old" and "out of step with [her] desires and [her] life as a young person". In this context, she says she doesn't "tell [her] parents anything about [her] life", as they are "in another world" and "don't understand her". Yet her parents - children of the baby boom - were in their twenties at the time of the "sexual revolution[26]" of the 1970s. At that time, the younger generation, whose motto was "liberate yourself from your elders and the old world[27]", was gradually breaking down the shackles in which sexuality was confined. But Anne-Sophie's parents' youth was different. Her mother grew up in a family "where the parish priest was important" and spent her entire school life in an institution, "with the nuns". She was 22 when she met Anne-Sophie's father, and married him less than a year later. Today, religion still plays an important role in her mother's life - "she watches mass on TV" - and the traditional values she acquired in her youth remain the order of the day. In conservative families, girls are the object of special attention - limited and controlled outings, supervised dating. This family (and social) control aims to delay their sexual debut as long as possible, in order to preserve their virtue and make them respectable wives[28].

"A smooth life, by the book"

In the traditional patriarchal family model, the sexual division of roles is firmly established, and parental authority is strong. Children - mainly girls - are expected to conform to their

---

26. TARNERO (Jacques), *Mai 68 - La révolution fiction*, Éditions Milan, Paris, 1998.
27. TARNERO (Jacques), *ibid*, p. 11.
28. BOZON (Michel), *op. cit.*

parents' upbringing[29]. Thus, when Anne-Sophie confided her dream of "becoming a policeman" to her parents as a teenager, they advised her to abandon this project on the grounds that "it's not for a girl!"

Ever since she was "a little girl", Anne-Sophie has obeyed her parents and "never rebelled", even if she has been "tempted" on several occasions. They want me to be responsible, but I'm responsible! I've got my driving license, my A-levels, I've always worked in the summer [...]", but that doesn't give her the right to go out without their authorization.

Outside her university hours, Anne-Sophie doesn't go out much: "I'm never allowed to go out, except to go to sports [...] for my mother, I'm always too young!" Her parents' reaction shows that they do not want their daughter's sexuality to become independent of the family institution and religious morality[30], and to be influenced by her friends' lifestyles. This ban on going out contributes - in a way - to isolating her from her peers and their practices, reinforcing the "gap" between her experience and that of her group of friends, as well as her feeling of being "left out": "I'm allowed to do things [to go out] always two years behind my friends [...] I've never been allowed to go and spend New Year's Eve with them! [...] Now, they don't even invite me anymore when there's a party or even just when they go for a walk [because] they know I couldn't go with them. [...] They have memories together, and I'm even more apart!" This situation accentuates the loneliness expressed by Anne-Sophie and the

---

29. Carnino (Guillaume), *Pour en finir avec le sexisme*, Éditions L'Échappée, Paris, 2005.
30. Bozon (Michel), *op. cit.*, p. 51.

fact that she has no one to talk to: "I feel alone! and all alone, you're useless! [...] I have no sister, no brother, and there's no one my age in my family! [...] I have no cousins..." In this context, it's not easy to express or form a concrete idea of sexuality. Yet in our society, sexuality appears to be a fundamental personal experience in the construction and identity of the subject[31].

Sexuality, a taboo subject

Contemporary sexuality is marked by the decline of its regulation by absolute principles such as sexual exclusivity, a limited number of partners before marriage, sex within the institution of marriage, etc.[32]. Moreover, sexuality today is marked by an earlier initiation of individuals, who learn - from the onset of puberty - practices of physical and relational exploration (kissing, deep kissing, caresses...) preceding sexual intercourse as such (genital penetration). According to H. Lagrange's study on "l'entrée dans la sexualité", the transition to genital sexuality "takes place over several years, and less and less with the same partner[33]". In this respect, the author points to the existence of an autonomous period of adolescent sexuality - dubbed the "flirtation period" - largely determined "by norms and models of conduct developed among peers[34]".

---

31. BOZON (Michel), *ibid.*, p. 31.

32. BOZON (Michel), *ibid.*, p. 42-43.

33. In France, in the mid-1990s, the first kiss took place at 14 for both boys and girls, while the first sexual intercourse took place at around 17 and a half; LAGRANGE (H.) "Le sexe apprivoisé ou l'intention du flirt", *Revue française de sociologie*, 1, 1998, p. 139-175, in: LAGRANGE (H.) et LHOMOND (B.) (dir.), *L'Entrée dans la sexualité. Le comportement des jeunes dans le contexte du sida*, Éditions La Découverte, Paris, 1997.

34. LAGRANGE (H.), *ibid.*

In Anne-Sophie's family, the subject of sexuality is never discussed, because for her parents, "sex is taboo". What's more, they can't imagine her having "a boyfriend" at her age. On this subject, Anne-Sophie tells me an anecdote that illustrates, in her opinion, her parents' "offbeat and completely naive" view of "the sexuality of today's youth". At the age of 19, she was watching a TV show with her parents. During the program[35], the presenter asked: "Out of 100 French teenagers, how many talk about sexuality with their parents?" Her mother looked at her with a smile and said: "You don't know about that, do you? It's not your age yet, you're too young!" For her parents - marked by the influence of religious morality - sexuality is always part of a certain set of principles.

Controlled sexuality

For conservatives, today's sexuality "leads to the sexual nomadism of individuals" and upsets the role of "women, who no longer know how to stay in their place[36]". Anne-Sophie's parents may not be so extreme, but they seem to share this point of view. In their view, their 21-year-old daughter is not yet "old enough" to have a love life. Similarly, sexuality needs to take shape in a "serious relationship" and not in a variety of more or less informed experiments. Finally, while their daughter's virginity may not seem essential, fidelity and marriage remain values to which they adhere. In this context, Anne-Sophie admits to having "a lot of trouble" getting her parents to

---

35. *Watch your step*, "[her] parents' favorite show", Anne-Sophie tells me in a mocking tone.

36. BOZON (Michel), *op. cit.,* p. 45.

understand that she'd like to "be like everyone else" - i.e. like her friends - and that it's "normal and not unhealthy" at her age "to have a boyfriend".

Unlike her group of friends, Anne-Sophie hasn't really experienced a "flirtation period". While the desire to have a boyfriend is certainly present, her rare outings leave her with very few opportunities to meet someone. In fact, she is forbidden "to bring a boy home".

When it comes to sexuality (excluding prostitution), Anne-Sophie has two experiences. The first was with "a nice boy" with whom "there was no sex", and the second was with a boy she was in love with and with whom she made love for the first time in September 2006. However, these two short stories left a bitter taste in her mouth, as she explains that she didn't feel comfortable or "really respected" in the relationship (mainly concerning her second story). Today, even if Anne-Sophie doesn't feel "up to it" and is apprehensive about having a boyfriend, she hopes to "meet someone" to "share and learn about love". In the meantime, her sexuality is based exclusively on prostitution.

Anne-Sophie began occasional prostitution at the end of November 2006. This practice, in stark contrast to the upbringing instilled in her by her parents, marks her desire to break away from "a strict and stifling upbringing". Her parents had a "very pejorative" image of prostitutes and clients, whom they described as "marginal, poor, lost and violent[37]". By prostituting

---

37. Before becoming a prostitute, Anne-Sophie also shared this view, but today she has changed her mind, noting that "both clients and escorts are normal people".

herself, Anne-Sophie comes up against family morality head-on. She also makes the connection with her upbringing, blaming her parents for her actions. We note, however, that she doesn't confront them directly, since her prostitution remains a secret. It's as if she's made a clear choice to distance herself from her family's morals, while protecting her parents.

3.2.2 *Prostitution as a means of escape*

For students who fit Anne-Sophie's profile, prostitution is seen as a means of emancipating themselves from family values and norms. By prostituting themselves, these students distance themselves from the parental model, marking their desire for autonomy in relation to their own. From this perspective, these students want to take charge of their lives - their intimate lives at any rate - and participate in the construction of their personal identity. In this respect, Annabelle's story - which echoes Anne-Sophie's - is our reference point.

I secure Annabelle's interview thanks to Michel - an escort client I interviewed a month earlier - who reassured her of my approach and intentions. Before the meeting, we exchange several emails, as well as a dozen Mp's. Annabelle said she was interested in my project and asked me several questions about my research.

I meet Annabelle at the entrance to the Palais des Congrès in Paris, where she is attending several conferences. We settle into the lobby of a quiet, chic hotel. Before starting the interview, Annabelle explains that she'd like to see more sources talking about "free prostitution" and highlighting the "fulfilling" nature of the activity, as she feels this posture suits her. The interview takes place in a pleasant atmosphere. Annabelle is at ease, and talks at length about her experience as a "libertine" prostitute[38]. She tells me she expects our interview to "shed new light" on her prostitution[39].

At the age of 24, Annabelle has a Master's 2 in Economics and is currently preparing to enter the civil service. After graduating, Annabelle moved back to the provinces to live with her parents, with whom she maintains "a good relationship". Throughout her schooling and to this day, her parents - both senior executives - support her. As a result, Annabelle has "never lacked for anything" and feels that "her life is pretty comfortable". Like her older brother, she was brought up with Catholic values - she attended private schools - and today considers herself "Catholic, but not practicing". Annabelle says she is "well surrounded", has "good friends" with whom she "shares the same interests" and is currently in "a serious love affair[40]".

---

38. During the interview, when Annabelle talks about her paid encounters, she uses innuendo. She never uses the explicit terms "prostitute" and "prostitution", and only once uses "escort" and "escorting". This shows how Annabelle views her prostitution. For her, it's more like "a libertine game".

39. Following the interview, we continue to communicate by e-mail and on the Forum, which will complete the analysis of his trajectory.

40. Unlike Anne-Sophie, Annabelle now enjoys a more fulfilling social life. Yet both were raised in traditional families. However, because of her studies, Annabelle lived away from home for four years, thus escaping family control more easily.

Prostitution as a guarantee of freedom

For Anne-Sophie and Annabelle, who grew up in families where the subject of sexuality was only mentioned in hushed tones, it can only take place within specific frameworks, i.e. "a man you love, with whom you marry, you don't sleep with if there's no love". In this context, their practice of prostitution enables them to have "a fulfilling sexuality", as well as a certain "independence".

Prostitution makes it possible to have several sexual partners, thus inscribing sexuality as "active" and "varied". Students like Anne-Sophie and Annabelle are looking for affection, sex and new experiences. Each partner brings a different "scenario" and contributes to "enriching" the escort experience. Quite often, these students have not had many sexual experiences during their teenage years, mainly because of strong parental control. In a way, prostitution allows them to "catch up" on the experiences they didn't have in their youth.

As far as Annabelle was concerned, school took over from family control, limiting the opportunities for flirtation: "well, I had a fairly classic sexuality, I mean... I didn't have an affair very, very young... It's probably because I went to Catholic schools and... *(smiles)* I don't know if you know, but it's not necessarily, well it doesn't encourage it!" When she left home to go to university in Paris, Annabelle "took flight" and became more involved in her own life. Of course, she was still heavily dependent on her parents - mainly financially - but she spent her time freely, without parental or institutional supervision. It is in this context of relative autonomy that she makes her first experiences of love, libertinism and then prostitution. For this type of student, living in a different type of accommodation from their parents gives them the opportunity to free themselves from family control over their daily lives[41]. In this context, they can adopt other attitudes and behaviors without fear of "shocking family morals", since it is now easier for them to hide part of their lives. In fact, most student escorts choose to keep this activity quiet, not only to avoid the judgment of their peers (and the rest of society), but also because it embodies the place where they alone determine the rules.

"To be free and independent"

For students like Annabelle, whose lives are still marked by a number of prohibitions, the secret practice of prostitution gives them a space all their own, a place where they alone have the right to see, where they alone are the judges of their actions. Through their prostitutional experiences, they can freely express their way of being - not in the open, of course, but at least to themselves. By setting themselves apart from family values, these students are helping to build their personal identity.

Annabelle has been secretly and occasionally prostituting herself for almost three years. She began "as a game, out of fantasy", as part of a libertine relationship. For around a year, her partner at the time introduced her to men "from her circle of friends", with whom she had occasional paid rendezvous. After their break-up, Annabelle resumed - after a break of several months - her venal encounters. This time, she was the only one to take the necessary steps, place an escort ad and select her

---

41. GALLAND (Olivier) and OBERTI (Marco), *op. cit.* p. 59.

clients. Today, Annabelle has four "regulars" and organizes around one meeting a month. Now that she's in a relationship, she'd like to stop escorting "out of respect for [her] lover", but explains that these meetings are part of "[her] balance" and in a way embody "[her] oxygen and [her] secret garden". For Annabelle's partner, sexual fidelity is an important principle. The fact of being in a couple means that he has to abide by certain rules, thus inviting him to abandon certain behaviors (in this case, prostitution). The couple, as an institution, plays a part in framing sexuality. Yet sexuality is precisely the place - perhaps the only place - where Annabelle can express herself fully, without any judgments. To take it away from her is, in a way, to take away part of her personal identity. That's why today she's so reluctant to stop prostituting: "I just can't stop, because when I decided to get involved with him, I really felt the need! It's really something that belongs to me alone, it's a bit like my oxygen, I really need it! It's really part of my life balance, in a general way...[...] I don't know if it's a desire for independence when I commit to someone, but I think there's a little bit of that anyway... *(smiles)* I don't like that, lying to him! But at the same time, I need to have my own life and... So it's a bit hard because sometimes I feel a little guilty and I say to myself he's a lovely guy... and I lie to him... I mean, I'm betraying him in a way, but I need to! And I know that maybe I wouldn't have got involved with him if I hadn't had this on the side, because I'd have been too scared..."

As a highly stigmatized activity[42], prostitution forces its players to keep this part of their lives secret, leading them to lie to their loved ones and lead a double life. For some student prostitutes, having a double life - and a prostitute's life at that - is a fantasy, especially for those who, like Annabelle, remain "unsuspected" by everyone.

Surpassing yourself and breaking the "forbidden" barrier

For student escorts at odds with traditional family values, prostitution is part of a certain fantasy. Without going into psychoanalysis, this fantasy stems mainly from a desire to "be someone else", to distance themselves from the image of the "well-behaved model girl" in which they are confined. By prostituting themselves, these students not only break away from their image, but also enter a dangerous territory, beyond the limits of what can be admitted. For these students, whose lives have more or less always been "smooth", prostitution "provides the spice" they seem to have lacked for a long time. What's more, prostitution allows them to go from Dr. Jekyll to Mr. Hyde without too much worry, if the secret is well kept. Being "someone else", they can let loose, push themselves and their limits. In this respect, Annabelle's testimony is truly enlightening: "I never imagined myself capable of doing that [prostituting myself]. I never thought I'd be able to do it on my own. And he [her partner in prostitution] had said to me, but above all, never go out on your own, because it's really dangerous... Well, he really warned me.

---

42. "Every activity has its share of stigmas, but prostitution has the most"; SCHAFF (Christelle), *op. cit.*, p. 74.

And so when I... I wanted to do it again because it's something that gives you a lot of thrills, it's really the adrenaline rush you're looking for afterwards! And I've already talked about it with a few people on the forum and it's a bit like a drug! Well, there's that... Well, you're scared of course, because you're, because it's delicate, because you're meeting someone you don't know, well... But at the same time, it's such a rich experience! *(laughs)* Well, in terms of sensations, I don't mean sexually at all, but just to go, at least for me, to go beyond oneself, finally to have a bit of another life, a taste for the forbidden and all that... Well, I really wanted to do it again, but it took many, many months before I made up my mind, because I was afraid, I was really afraid, I didn't know how to do it..."

Revealing your "dark side"

Prostitution is not a harmless practice. It carries a strong stigma, leading to a certain "degradation[43]" of the person who engages in this activity. In this context, students who resemble Annabelle's profile express their darker side, not only as venal women, but also as liars and manipulators. This hidden life offers them the opportunity to exercise power - the power to know - over people (their parents in particular) who believe they know everything about them. This power provides an "internal jubilation", a feeling of power, and is, in a way, revenge for "the deprivation of freedom". In this regard, Annabelle explains that "when you're used to leading a double life, because you are, when you lie to your parents, your boyfriend, your friends... It's,

---

43. CHALEIL (Max), *Prostitution - Le désir mystifié*, Éditions l'Aventurine, Paris, 2002, p. 555.

I don't know, it's really, it's exciting actually! To do things that people don't think you're capable of, to know it, but only you, to have little moments of internal jubilation like that when you broach the subject *(laughs)*... well... I don't really know... I don't really know how to explain it... Maybe it's also, I think that's really what it's all about too, the desire for a little bit of independence in relation to that and to create your own double life, my double which is at the same time me since I'm behaving well... Inventing another life too, yes, I think that's part of it too..."

Through prostitution, student escorts - like Anne-Sophie and Annabelle - demonstrate their desire to "break out of the shackles" of their families. For these students, who have always obeyed their parents' expectations, prostitution - as a hidden practice - is the place where they can be actors and masters of their actions. However, these young women do not reject the entirety of their upbringing, and certain values - fidelity and love, for example - still have a place in their discourse[44]. For other students, on the other hand, promises of love and fidelity are nothing but lies and illusions. This is what we'll see in the third and final pattern of ruptures.

---

44. Anne-Sophie, who declares that she lives her prostitution positively, is nevertheless wary of "[getting] emotionally involved in the relationship [because she has] no desire to [get] attached to a person who goes to whores!" Ideally, she imagines her future "married to a faithful man who loves me, of course!

3.3 DISILLUSIONMENT WITH LOVE

In the preface to Francesco Albertoni's book, we read that love is an experience "that we all know, having experienced it at least once[45]". Love is indeed a quest that all human beings share, and to which all aspire[46]. "We hope for it, we endure it, we mourn it", adds the Italian sociologist, yet falling in love is not a matter of chance, and can be understood as a social fact, responding to a certain number of rules and practices. In all cases, love occupies an important place in the social space and life of each individual. Claire - whose trajectory we will now analyze - explains that it is "the desire to love and be loved that drives [her]".

3.3.1 A shaken vision of love

In the discourse of student escorts, love is a recurring theme. However, their vision and representations of this phenomenon are marked by a certain "fatalism" and bitterness. In this respect, Claire's experience is exemplary.

---

45. ALBERTONI (Francesco), *Le Choc amoureux*, Éditions Ramsay, Paris, 1981, p. 9.

46. According to German author and journalist Eric Hegmann, "today, the search for love is more popular than ever [and] the Internet has become the number one matchmaker". Indeed, the number of dating sites on the Net and the number of users of these services continues to grow. Among our European neighbors, there are over 2,000 German dating sites and over 6.2 million registered users (twice as many as in 2003). Germany has almost 11 million singles; GIESE (Annika), "L'amour à portée de mulot", *Journal Europa*, July-August 2007, p. 11.

Following the comment that Bertrand - an occasional escort client - posted on my topic the day after our meeting[47], Claire contacted me via mp and offered to meet her.

We meet as agreed near a metro station. Claire is dressed as she told me in her message the day before, which is to say rather soberly: dark pants, blue T-shirt and long black coat. She wears no make-up or jewelry. She smiles and greets me with a kiss.

Claire has only two hours to spare, so she goes ahead and chooses the restaurant where we sit down for lunch. It's not the ideal place to conduct an interview, but on the whole, the interview goes well. Claire is a friendly young woman who's quite at ease: she calls me by my first name, asks me questions about my tastes, my life, jokes... as if we'd known each other for some time already. As soon as we're seated, she wants us to get to the heart of the matter and doesn't ask me to explain anything further, either about my approach or what I'm going to do with her interview. Claire answers each of my questions at some length. During the interview, she occasionally lowers her voice several times - mainly when she explicitly mentions her prostitution - to prevent our tablemates from overhearing what she's saying. After the interview, I offer to meet her again at another time. She agrees and undertakes to organize "a friendly get-together" to which Sandrine - whom Claire wants to get to know - would be invited. We communicate regularly

------

47. Message from Bertrand on my topic: "I met [Eva] last night for a drink, and she put me through a tough questionnaire. *She's a nice young woman, who's looking for testimonials for her dissertation. Unlike a chat, there wasn't really much exchange, but she knows how to ask pertinent, thought-provoking questions. I hope I was of some help to her, while her questions opened up new avenues of thought for me. It was interesting, and I encourage volunteers to come forward! (PS: journalists of all stripes looking for racy testimonials, this is not for you...).*

by mp, and we meet again twice: with Sandrine a month later, then at the JAD in June.

Claire is 26 and in the final year of her biology thesis. At the age of 17, she left for Germany, where she took her baccalauréat at the Lycée Français de Berlin, "a semi-private school with a fairly high standard and children from good families". Claire, for her part, comes from an "average" family living in a "godforsaken village" in eastern France. Her father runs a "small business" there, and her mother, having lost her job following their divorce, is now an accountant "in a small company". Claire has lived away from home since her final year of high school, but maintains a "good relationship" with her parents, whom she "calls just about every week". After her year in Berlin, she moved to Paris and enrolled in a preparatory class, before entering a renowned engineering school. At the end of her DEA, Claire was awarded a "scholarship from the Ministry" - 1,180 euros net per month - to finance her thesis. Since becoming a doctoral student, Claire has been self-supporting and independent of her family.

At the moment, Claire has "a regular lover", but doesn't intend to continue this relationship, as she "doesn't see any point" in it. She says she's not in love, but can't bear the idea of lying to this "lover", especially about her paid sex life. According to her, "lying is perhaps even worse than cheating!" When it comes to "cheating", Claire calls herself an "expert", referring to what her parents and, by extension, herself, have experienced.

While married, Claire's father had "several mistresses". When she was 14, he left his wife and children and "rebuilt his life with his mistress, who is now his wife". At the time - and still today - Claire had a very difficult time with her parents' divorce.

According to her, the separation "shattered [her] family[48]" and with it her ideals of "love always". For Claire, love "without deceit" and fidelity in marriage are decoys: "in any case, men inevitably cheat on their wives, they go elsewhere and so on. You see, I already have a vision of fidelity that's quite... *(smile)* shaken[49]!" And when she's in a relationship herself, she finds it hard to trust her partner. Yet Claire has had "several great [love] stories", each lasting two years. However, she gives the impression that she didn't really "blossom" through these relationships, as she confides that she didn't really feel "desired" by her partner: "But hey, I know you're desired when you're desired by your boyfriend, but hey, it's not the same! It's not purely desire because there's love and... Well, love makes you blind so... it's not, it's not really desire! Maybe he [the lover] imagines another [girl] when he looks at you, we don't know! *(laughs)*" Through her speech, we understand that for Claire, the feeling of love doesn't seem sincere because it's "blind". In this case, there's no point in having a relationship, or it's not worth it, because it's not "well-founded". Disappointed by her unions, Claire decides to give up the quest for love and focus solely on desire - "pure desire" - that is, free of amorous feeling.

---

48. Not only did Claire no longer see her father on a daily basis, but her mother also found herself unemployed, as she worked in a business with him.

49. In this respect, prostitution reinforces her convictions. When I ask her what she dislikes most about her customers, Claire replies: "that they cheat and lie to their wives".

Disappointing "free" relationships

After having been involved in "three big stories", then a few shorter "serious relationships", Claire decided to try "adventures with men passing through". She sought out her "one-night stands" via an Internet dating site. In this way, Claire meets several men with whom she has sexual relations without remuneration. In such relationships, she says she becomes aware that "[her] body is desirable" and learns at the same time "[to] feel like a woman". However, libertine relationships leave her with "a bitter taste", and in the end, she once again feels unsatisfied: "So I've been having adventures with casual men for about a year now. And at the same time, I'm having a great time sexually, but on a human level, sometimes there's been a real lack of sharing! The sex was fine, but afterwards, well, bof! It was all about the sex! Sometimes, I had the impression that the guy didn't give a damn, that he had no respect... It turned me on to have sex with guys I didn't know, but in the end it was pretty shitty... [...] And if I'm going to have sex for sex's sake, I might as well get paid for it! *(laughs)*" These women - whom Sylvie Bigot calls "the sentimentally disillusioned[50]" - can't be satisfied with "one-night stands", because they expect a more lasting commitment from their partner. They expect the "free lover" to give them some form of recognition - through gestures, words or even "gifts" - for having accepted to "offer" themselves freely. According to Claire, if men lack respect, it's above all "because it costs them nothing!"

---

50. BIGOT (Sylvie), *op. cit.*

From now on, Claire no longer wants to get involved in a "serious" relationship, as she fears "being cheated [and] betrayed", nor in "one-night stands" where respect and consideration are too often lacking. For all that, she has no wish to give up her sex life. After more than a year and a half of Internet libertinism, Claire decided to trade in her "one-night stands" for paid sex. Since October 2006, Claire has been advertising as an escort on a specialized website, and has been prostituting herself on an occasional basis - one or two dates a month. In addition to the financial aspect, these encounters bring her, in her words, "respect" and "self-esteem".

3.3.2 Prostitution as a source of self-respect and self-esteem

When Claire embarked on her escorting career, she was looking to fill an emotional and sexual void. Disappointed by her previous love affairs and libertine relationships, she no longer wants to get involved in "that kind of story", but wishes to maintain her sexual activity, and improve her sexuality by learning new practices and experiences. In this context, her practice of prostitution makes sense.

Money in the sexual relationship clarifies the situation. Student escorts who fit Claire's profile know that the escort encounter will not go beyond the terms of the contract, and that it's pointless to expect "a story" beyond the venal rendez-vous. In this context, the latter can live the encounter intensely without worrying about the future. And that's how Claire sees paid relationships: "Escorting actually provides a framework, there are limits! For example, my client last night, well, he said I'm paying you so that... [...] Well, it was clear! I know why he's paying me, he knows why he's paying me and that's that! And he told me, it's clear I'm never going to leave my wife, and I don't want him to leave his wife. There's a kind of code of ethics [...] since he's a customer, I'll never call him at home! because there are rules... And neither will he, he's not supposed to call me at any time. I don't have the same relationship with a customer as with another guy. But you see, in the moment, you don't think about it, and for two hours you've forgotten that you're in a sexual relationship, and you're having a great time! Many of her fondest sexual memories have taken place in the context of a paid relationship. The encounters were gratifying, as they were erotically fulfilling: "it's better when it's paid for [...] you get more respect than for a one-night stand".

Self-esteem and self-confidence

When we talked about Claire's "love breakdowns", we pointed out that she hadn't felt "considered" in her free relationships. On the other hand, she says she feels "respected" and "valued" in her paid relationships.

The type of customers she meets plays a significant role in this sense of self-esteem. As we saw in the second part of the study, the clients of student escorts belong, for the most part, to the upper social classes and know how to demonstrate a certain "education". In this context, the fact that "respectable men" are willing to pay to spend a moment with "ordinary girls", i.e. without any mark of distinction, accentuates the feeling of recognition to which the latter aspire.

Money also plays a crucial role in the student escorts' sense of self-worth, as it offers a kind of concrete "value" to their companionship - companionship they previously gave away for free. In this regard, Claire explains that "escorting [has] made me realize [my] value": "I'm at your service, you're not in love with me, you're having fun in my arms ok... But in this case, you're paying me! [...] In fact, I've come to understand that I give them [men] a lot, and sometimes I say to myself that some of them were lucky to find a girl like me, because most girls are a lot more uptight [...] they're not as comfortable, they need a lot of time... And you see, I've come to understand that this has value! [...] What I used to give them [in free relationships], that had value, and that meant they [the men] had something I didn't, which was money, so maybe I could find some common ground! *(laughs)*" Claire's discourse gives the impression that she is making her customers pay for the disappointments she has suffered with the men with whom she has had gratuitous relationships. In this context, prostitution embodies a kind of revenge on the male gender, repairing the "damage" felt during free sex. In this way, Claire inverts - in a way - the mechanisms of gender domination usually at work in the act of prostitution[51]. Through her words, we get the feeling that it is she - the woman - who has the power over her clients - the men, since she chooses them. And yet, even if Claire's practice of prostitution seems to attenuate relations of domination, they are not absent.

On the other hand, we know that the fees charged by student escorts are relatively high - especially in view of their budget. From this point of view, the amount the customer is willing to pay already confers a certain value on the escort; and the higher the amount, the more the escort feels valued. The extract from

---

51. Please refer to the first sub-section - "A complex theme imbued with strong ideologies" - in the first part of this study (p. 21).

Claire's interview illustrates this point: "But I mean, there are men who are willing to pay for you! These relationships are really rewarding. He told me I was beautiful, he wanted me like crazy and he gave me money! You know, you feel like the king of the world! And that's really rewarding, that's for sure. Not only do we do it respectfully, but we also give you a relatively large sum of money… so yes, it's rewarding."

For some student escorts, prostitution also helps to reconcile them with their bodies. Jean Baudrillard states that in our society, "beauty has become, for women, an absolute imperative[52]". Student escorts - like many other people, men and women alike - have internalized this social "norm". In this context, many of them talk about body complexes. Having customers - i.e. "men willing to pay" to spend an intimate moment with them (and by extension with their bodies) - reassures them of their seductive power. Feeling "beautiful" and "desired", their confidence is reinforced. Like Claire and Sandrine - who have long been self-conscious about their bodies - these escorts now know that they can use their charms to please others (in this case, men). This power boosts their self-esteem. They can now fully assume themselves as women and show themselves "as [they are]".

In this context, escorting contributes to the sexual equilibrium and personal fulfillment of students like Claire. In this respect, Sylvie Bigot analyzes that this type of woman - those who experience their prostitution in a positive light - is "at the

---

52. BAUDRILLARD (Jean), *La Société de consommation - Ses mythes, ses structures*, Éditions Denoël, Paris, 1970, p. 206.

opposite end of the spectrum from those for whom getting paid is an affront to their dignity[53]".

A practice that takes the pressure off

Here's an extract from Sandrine's interview, illustrating how prostitution reconciled her with her body.

"I'm more comfortable!... Yeah, I think that's something that's changed. Well, actually, before I started [prostituting myself], it might sound weird, weird to say that I'm doing this when I was super-complexed, super-sad about myself, convinced that I couldn't please anyone except a few sick people *(shared laughter)*... who must have really had a problem! In fact, when I put my ad on the site, I took some photos of myself, you know, with the self-timer and all... but they really didn't do me any favors! More of my body, because I didn't put my face on, but they showed me as I really am... And I thought I'd see if people would want to see that [her body]! Because when you're not too comfortable in your own skin and all that... That was also part of my approach at the start. I didn't necessarily think it would lead to anything, you know! And then, when you do it and, an hour later, you've already received a bunch of messages... Wouaaaouh! you think, there's something there! *(smile)*. But even now, of course, when you're with a customer, you're spending time together, you're both naked, and I think that helps me feel a lot more at ease. You see, before, even with... even with my lover *(smile)*, I know I used to get dressed quickly, when we were in bed, I didn't like staying naked next to him, that's all... Now I have a rather... easier relationship with nudity! In other words, no more problems! I'm more obsessed by what he can see, the little fat rolls... *(laughs)*".

---

53. BIGOT (Sylvie), *op. cit.*

Being "useful"

Student escorts give meaning to their practice of prostitution by evoking its "useful" character; useful to the institution of the couple and marriage; useful "to frustrated men".

Like Claire[54] - whose parents' divorce left its mark on her - student escorts emphasize that their prostitution contributes to the durability of the union of couples (married or not)[55]. Whereas a mistress can "break up a couple", the prostitute guarantees the couple's equilibrium, since she doesn't seek to develop amorous feelings towards the men who pay her. This is why Bertrand - a client of occasional escorts - uses escorts: "Well, I'm very happy in a couple, with my family... Yes, with my family, because I've got children... I don't want to break that up at all, and in a way... I'd say that the venal encounter is the minimum risk. In the sense that there's no risk of attachment... There's no... Well, we meet, I'd say on a certain level, for something very specific at a very specific time under very specific conditions... There, there! *(smile)* So that's it... I'd say that I forbid myself, and even within

---

54. By prostituting herself, Claire chooses to be the one you sleep with - even without feeling -, rather than the one you cheat on and lie to. But she can't stand the idea of playing the role of "mistress", because "[she] knows exactly how it feels! In this situation, prostitution seems the most legitimate alternative in Claire's eyes. As a prostitute, she is able to enjoy a non-committal sex life within a precise framework - money circumscribes the relationship - thus avoiding the role of "homewrecker".

55. Let's quote an extract from Sandrine's speech: "But maybe, by coming to see me, they [the men] will, so they'll come to see me, with me, it's clear it's defined and all, rather than going to see the secretary with whom it's going to be tendentious, it can destroy their couple and all... like that... I mean, I have the impression that I'm not endangering couples whatsoever, I'm not endangering people's lives, I'm not hurting anyone! (smiles).

venal encounters, I forbid myself that it becomes a lover-lover relationship... There's no loving feeling, but there's a certain form of friendship!"

Several student escorts also mention that, without them, some men "would surely be frustrated!" Frustrated, in particular, because the sexuality they have with their wives is "not very fulfilling" and the pleasure is "not often there". And yet, we live in a society that advocates sexual fulfillment. In such a context, being able to give your partner pleasure is a valued and rewarding behavior. A "good" lover is "one who knows how to bring pleasure to the other[56]". In this respect, Sandrine explains that she helps to "boost the ego" of some of her customers by proving to them that they can "give pleasure to a woman", since she herself is "receptive to the pleasure he [the customer] wants to give [her]".

In these situations, student escorts - like prostitutes in general - take on the role of "caretakers", underlining the legitimacy of their prostitutional practice. Yet for many thinkers - feminists in particular - attributing a social utility to prostitution helps to "normalize" (i.e., make acceptable) this practice, giving it a "natural" and therefore immutable character. We know, however, that there's nothing natural about the prostitution system - it's a social fact - since it's based on complex, socially instituted mechanisms. These mechanisms obey the "established order" (i.e., the prevailing social structure and system of norms), which itself lies at the heart of relations of domination.

---

56. BIGOT (Sylvie), *op. cit.*

*

* *

As we've seen, students who prostitute themselves do so of their own free will and on their own terms. While this choice is a personal one, it is also - like all choices - part of a particular context. Prostitution doesn't happen by chance. The need for money - highlighted by Sandrine's story - the desire to get away from it all - analyzed from Anne-Sophie and Annabelle's point of view - or disappointment in love relationships - made explicit by Claire's experience - are not enough on their own to explain why some students turn to prostitution.

According to a study on "the risk of prostitution among young people[57]", there is a "basic terrain" in which "germinates" a certain number of dysfunctions - linked to the personal and social history of individuals - which lead certain young people into prostitution. The survey shows that these "dysfunctions" are varied and self-influencing. They can include "biographical accidents" (physical, moral and sexual violence), problems of identity and identification with parental models, social isolation, psychological fragility, social disqualification by the family to which they belong, distorted social representations of modes of success, or the fact of having - in their network - acquaintances belonging to the world of prostitution.

---

57. This study, carried out by a French association, does not refer to the student public, but targets young people aged 18 to 25 who are being monitored by social services and are in situations of economic and social precariousness. Although the profile of these young people does not really correspond to that of student escorts, it does echo that of Julien ; ANRS - Service insertion jeunes - Association nationale de réadaptation sociale, *Le risque prostitutionnel chez les jeunes de 18-25 ans* (étude exploratoire), Paris, 1995.

The choice of prostitution is therefore not the fruit of a single element, but rather of a combination of various personal and social ruptures, of varying degrees of severity. Paradoxically, prostitution becomes an alternative that gives meaning to the practices and life choices of our interviewees.

Students' "passage à l'acte" into prostitution takes place in a particular context, at a particular time in their lives, and for some seems to be a way out of a difficult situation. However, no studies have been carried out to track the progress of these people, or to assess the consequences - both individual and social - that these practices may have in the long term.

CONCLUSION

In addition to the difficulties of approaching those involved in student prostitution, and of being accepted as a sociologist within this milieu, working on this theme was not easy, as it is sometimes difficult to remain objective on a theme so imbued with ideologies and issues. Moreover, as Sylvie Bigot points out, any work on sexuality involves controversy and is not always well accepted or well received. Sexuality is still regarded as a less than noble field for sociological investigation. Nevertheless, the subject is no less relevant and interesting.

This study has shown us that there is no single form of prostitution. Student escorts, by virtue of the specificity of their prostitution practices, constitute a category in their own right in this field. However, we have also come to understand that the careers of these students - like those of other prostitutes - are marked by a series of ruptures that lead them to choose prostitution.

It should also be noted that student prostitution is not a homogeneous reality. Julien's experience - the only male prostitute in the survey - is a reminder of this. What's more, while all our female students declare that they experience prostitution positively, it's not certain that all students who have made this choice share this point of view, nor that our respondents will retain this vision in their future. It would be interesting to see Sandrine, Claire, Anne-Sophie, Annabelle and Julien again in a few years' time, with this in mind.

Similarly, this study focuses on a particular form of student prostitution, carried out via the Internet, and whose players are all Forum regulars. Yet prostitution venues are as diverse as the forms of prostitution themselves. In this context, it would be advisable to broaden the fields of investigation of student prostitution to include hostess bars, massage parlors, the street...

Finally, this study also reveals a certain social malaise. Although our respondents claim to be fulfilled in this activity and to have chosen it of their own free will, we have seen that this "choice" is at the heart of social relationships where male and economic domination reign. Faced with this state of affairs, we can only hope for a change in mentality to stem the tide of inequality. We know that education is one of the keys to changing mentalities. Yet the resources deployed by public authorities remain insufficient. As a result, some associations are trying to fill this gap. This was one of the aims of my internship with the Mouvement du Nid delegation in Nantes. Aware that information and prevention are essential to "getting things moving", this association asked me to find the most appropriate medium for talking to students about student prostitution, within a preventive framework[1]. To do this, I distributed 180 questionnaires on the Nantes campus to second-year psychology and medicine students. Thanks to this internship, I learned a lot, both professionally and personally. I had to find a place for myself within a team of activists that had been in place for several years; learn to assert my skills and points of view; bring a project to fruition and do my best to meet the organization's expectations.

While this quantitative survey has shed light on a number of issues, as has this dissertation, the subject of student prostitution is far from exhausted and remains too little known.

---

1. However, it is essential to question the manner (tone, form...) in which prevention should be approached. As prostitution is a "delicate" subject, covering a wide range of realities, it's important to carefully weigh up what is being said, and the consequences of such prevention. Before any preventive action can be taken, it seems to me essential to gain a better understanding of the subject - and therefore to pursue and expand research on this topic. In addition, it would be interesting to cooperate with various competent bodies and organizations in the field: students' unions, university doctors, CROUS, associations with different positions on prostitution, etc., in order to offer a more "global" and therefore more "complete" vision of the phenomenon.

BIBLIOGRAPHY

■ Books and articles used for the methodology

BEAUD (Stéphane) and WEBER (Florence), *Guide de l'enquête de terrain - Produire et analyser des données ethnographiques*, Éditions La Découverte, Paris, 1998, 328 p.

FAVRET-SAADA (Jeanne), *Les mots, la mort, les sorts - Sorcellerie contemporaine dans le Bocage de l'Ouest*, Éditions Gallimard, 1977, 424 p.

HUMPHREYS (Laud), *Le Commerce des pissotières - Pratiques homosexuelles anonymes dans l'Amérique des années 1960*, Paris XIII, Éditions La Découverte, 2007, 199 p.

PINSON (Michel) and PINSON-CHARLOT (Monique), *Voyage en grande bourgeoisie - Journal d'enquête*, PUF, Paris, 2005 (2nd updated edition - 1st ed. 1997), 186 p.

SCHWARTZ (Olivier), *Le Monde privé des ouvriers - Hommes et femmes du Nord*, PUF, Paris, 1990, 531 p.

WEBER (Florence), Principes de méthodes (Chapitre I), in: *Le travail à côté*, INRA/EHESS éditions, Paris, 1989.

WEBER (Florence), Vers une auto-analyse (Chapter II), in: *Le travail à côté*, INRA/EHESS éditions, Paris, 1989.

■ References on prostitution

→ *Non-student prostitution*

ANRS - Service insertion jeunes - Association nationale de réadaptation sociale, *Le risque prostitutionnel chez les jeunes de 18-25 ans* (étude exploratoire), Paris, 1995.

Archives générales du royaume de Belgique, *Des étuves aux eros centers - Prostitution et traite des femmes du Moyen Âge à nos jours*. Brussels, 1995, 118 pp.

ADLER (Laure), *Les maisons closes 1830-1930 - La vie quotidienne*, Hachette Littératures, 2003, 247 p.

BOUAMAMA (Saïd), *L'homme en question - Le processus du devenir-client de la prostitution*. Paris, 2004.

CHALEIL (Max), *Prostitution - Le désir mystifié*, Éditions l'Aventurine, Paris, 2002, 641 p.

DUPONT-MONOD (Clara), *Histoire d'une prostituée*, Éditions Grasset & Fasquelle, Paris, 2003, 178 p.

LEGARDINIER (Claudine), *La Prostitution*, Éditions Milan, Paris, 1996, 63 p.

LEGARDINIER (Claudine), *Prostitution - 100 mots pour comprendre*, Mouvement du Nid, Clichy, 2005, 71 p.

LEGARDINIER (Claudine) and BOUAMAMA (Saïd), *Les Clients de la prostitution : l'enquête*, Presses de la Renaissance, Paris, 2006, 268 p.

NIKITA (Maîtresse) and SCHAFFAUSER (Thierry), *Fières d'être putes*, Éditions l'Altiplano, Paris, 2007, 123 p.

NOR (Malika), *La Prostitution*, Éditions Le Cavalier Bleu, Paris, 2001, 125 p.

MOSSUZ-LAVAU (Janine) and HANDMAN (Marie-Élisabeth), *La Prostitution à Paris*, Éditions de la Martinière, Paris, 2005, 365 p.

PETHERSON (Gail), Prostitution II - in: HIRATA (N.), LABORIE (F.), LE DAORE (H.) et SENOTIER (D.) *Dictionnaire critique du féminisme*, 2000, 2nd extended edition, PUF, 263 p.

SCHAFF (Christelle), *Prostitution en France : l'enquête*, Éditions de la Lagune, 2007, 200 p.

SOLE (Jacques), *L'Âge d'or de la prostitution - de 1879 à nos jours*, Plon, Paris, 1994, 667 p.

→ *Internet prostitution and student prostitution*

AHMED-CHAOUCH (Azzedine), "Elles se prostituent pour financer leurs études", *Aujourd'hui en France*, January 1st, 2007, p. 14.

ANONYMOUS, "Elles vendent leurs corps pour payer leurs études", *Entrevue* (mensuel), December 2006 (monthly), no. 173, p. 96-101.

BIGOT (Sylvie), *L'épanouissement sexuel des femmes au travers de l'escorting : mythe ou réalité ?* Journée regards insolites sur la sexualité - Regards artistiques et sociologiques sur la sexualité, Paris - École normale supérieure, June 2, 2007.

BONNEFOUS (Bastien), "À la fac de la précarité, option tapin", *Le 20 Minutes*, November 23, 2006, p. 6.

FRANCHON (Matthieu) and BITESNICH (Andreas), "Salariées le jour, escort girls la nuit", *Choc* (hebdomadaire), June 28 2007, n° 87, p. 26-33.

LOVE (Sacha), *Escort girl, le récit d'une double vie*, Alban Éditions, Paris, 2006, 129 p.

PHILIBERT (Jean-Marc), "La prostitution gagne les bancs de la fac", *Le Figaro*, October 30, 2006, p. 11.

PHILIPPE (E.), "Étudiante, je me suis prostituée", *Esprit Femme* (mensuel), February 2007, no. 21, pp. 56-57.

PHILIPPE (E.) and ADJOVI (L.), "Malaise dans l'université : étudiantes le jour, prostituées la nuit", *Jasmin* (hebdomadaire), Nov. 27, 2006, no. 6, pp. 10-13.

REUZEAU (Yann), *Les Débutantes - Prostituées en quelques clics*, play, 2006, performed from November 2006 to February 2007 at La Manufacture des Abbesses in Paris, seen January 18, 2007.

▪ General works

→ *Social relationships*

ALBERTONI (Francesco), *Le Choc amoureux*, Éditions Ramsay, Paris, 1981, 185 p.

BAUDRILLARD (Jean), *La Société de consommation - Ses mythes, ses structures*, Éditions Denoël, Paris, 1970, 318 p.

BERNFELD (Karin), *Alice au pays des femelles*, Éditions Balland, 2001, 314 p.

BOURDIEU (Pierre), *La Distinction - Critique sociale du jugement*, Les Éditions de Minuit, Paris, 1979, 670 p.

ERNAUX (Annie), *La Place*, Gallimard, Paris, 1983, 113 p.

GAULEJAC (Vincent De), *La Névrose de classe - Trajectoire sociale et conflit d'identité*, Hommes & Groupes Éditeurs, Paris, 1987, 298 p.

GAULEJAC (Vincent De), *L'Histoire en héritage - Roman familial et trajectoire sociale*, Éditions Desclée de Brouwer, Paris, 1999, 222 p.

GIESE (Annika), "L'amour à portée de mulot", *Journal Europa*, July-August 2007, p. 11.

LARDELLIER (Pascal), *Le Cœur NET - Célibat et amour sur le Web*, Éditions Belin, Paris, 2004, 251 p.

MOSSUZ-LAVAU (Janine), *L'Argent et nous*, Éditions de la Martinière, Paris, 2007, 365 p.

TARNERO (Jacques), *Mai 68 - La révolution fiction*, Éditions Milan, Paris, 1998, 63 p.

→ *Gender relations*

BOURDIEU (Pierre), *La Domination masculine*, Éditions du Seuil, Paris, 1998, 177 p.

BOZON (Michel), *Sociologie de la sexualité*, Armand Colin, 2005, 125 p.

CARNINO (Guillaume), *Pour en finir avec le sexisme*, Éditions L'Échappée, Paris, 2005, 126 p.

DELPHY (Christine), *L'Ennemi principal* (tome I), Éditions Syllepses, Paris, 1998.

LAGRANGE (H.), "Le sexe apprivoisé ou l'intention du flirt", *Revue française de sociologie*, 1, 1998, p. 139-175, in: LAGRANGE (H.) et LHOMOND(B.) (dir.), *L'entrée dans la sexualité. Le comportement des jeunes dans le contexte du sida*, Éditions La Découverte, Paris, 1997.

LAQUEUR (Thomas), *La Fabrique du sexe - Essai sur le corps et le genre en Occident*, Éditions Gallimard, Paris, 1992, 216 p.

TABET (Paola), "La grande arnaque: l'expropriation de la sexualité des femmes", in Actuel Marx, *Les Rapports sociaux de sexe*, no. 30, 2001, pp. 131-152.

→ *Student world*

BEAUD (Stéphane), *80 % au bac... et après ?*, Éditions La Découverte, Paris, 2003, 314 p.

BOUDON (Raymond), *L'Inégalité des chances - La mobilité sociale dans les sociétés industrielles*, Éditions Armand Colin, Paris, 1979, 334 p.

BOURDIEU (Pierre), *La Noblesse d'état - Grandes Écoles et esprit de corps*, Les Éditions de Minuit, Paris, 1989, 567 p.

BOURDIEU (Pierre) and PASSERON (Jean-Claude), *Les Héritiers: les étudiants de la culture*, Les Éditions de Minuit, Paris, 1964, 189 p.

DAURIAC (Jean-François), *Note de synthèse du rapport au ministre de l'Éducation nationale de la Recherche et de la Technologie sur la mise en œuvre du plan social étudiant*, Paris, 2000.

GALLAND (Olivier) and OBERTI (Marco), *Les Étudiants*, Éditions La Découverte, Paris, 1996, 118 p.

GRIGNON (Claude), *Les étudiants en difficulté : pauvreté et précarité - Rapport au ministre de la Jeunesse, de l'Éducation nationale et de la Recherche*, Paris, 2003.

WAUQUIEZ (Laurent), *Les aides aux étudiants: comment relancer l'ascenseur social*, Paris, 2006.

→ *Deviance*

BECKER (Howard S.), *Outsiders - Études de sociologie de la déviance*, Éditions A-M. Métailié, Paris, 1985, 248 p.

GOFFMAN (Erving), *Stigmate - Les usages sociaux des handicaps*, Les Éditions de Minuit, Paris, 1975, 175 p.

→ *Relationship to the body*

DARMON (Muriel), *Devenir anorexique - une approche sociologique*, Éditions La Découverte, Paris, 2003, 346 p.

▪ Websites consulted

- Observatory of Student Life (OVE) [03/29/2007], http://www.ove-national.education.fr/doc_lib/c346_rapport_precarite_2003.pdf
- Wikipedia, the free encyclopedia [07/23/2007], http://fr.wikipedia.org/wiki/Prostitution
Wikipedia, the free encyclopedia [07/23/2007], http://fr.wikipedia.org/wiki/Histoire prostitution
- FASTI (Fédération des associations de solidarité avec les travailleurs immigrés) [15/05/2007], *http://www.fasti.org/article.php3* ?id_article=403
Report: "Prostitution: the exploitation of foreign women" - Minutes of the national forum held on April 2, 2005.

▪ Filmography and audio-visual documents

MARSHALL (Gary), *Pretty Woman*, 1990 (USA).
SERREAU (Coline), *Chaos*, 2001 (France).
TÉCHINÉ André, *J'embrasse pas*, 1991 (France).
Report broadcast on *Envoyé spécial* (France 2): "Les occasionnelles de la prostitution", November 23, 2006.

APPENDICES

APPENDIX 1:

CONCEPTUAL MODEL OF THE PROSTITUTIONAL SYSTEM APPLIED TO STUDENT PROSTITUTES

In order to gain a better understanding of the mechanisms underlying student prostitution, I drew inspiration from the conceptual model invented by Sirma Bilge[1]. In a dynamic, multi-dimensional process, this model highlights the various relations of domination in place within the prostitutional system.

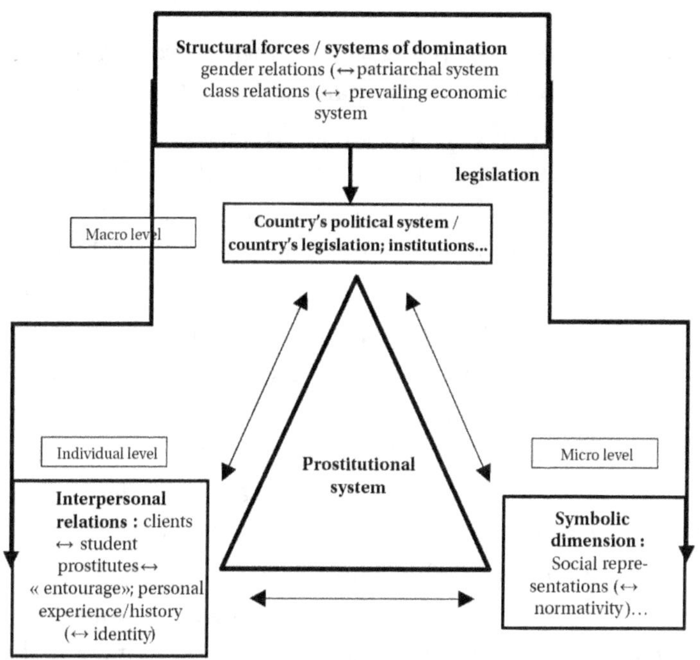

---

1. Sirma BILGE, a sociologist, was one of my professors at the Université de Montréal. During the "Migration, Ethnicity and Urban Diversity" course, she introduced the students (including me) to this conceptual model, which she used for her work on "Montreal's Turkish community".

APPENDIX 2:

INTERNET PROSTITUTION JARGON

Terms followed by an * are those used *exclusively on the* Forum.

Black-list: List of non-recommended clients - because they are violent, bad payers, unhygienic, discourteous... - that escorts distribute among themselves.

Escort = "escort" (or *"escort"; "escort-girl"; "escort-boy"*): Originally, escorting was the paid activity of accompanying a person to a restaurant, theater, business meeting, etc. In this context, the sexual relationship is not part of the contract and, if there is an act, it's a private matter. New means of communication (mainly the Internet) have changed this, and while there are still escorts who only accompany (they often work for agencies), the term is now used to designate all those who prostitute themselves on a regular or occasional basis, independently or on behalf of others, by soliciting on the Web. Contact between the customer and the escort is established over the Net (by e-mail, chat, etc., often followed by telephone), and includes setting the terms of the meeting. The escort can meet at home (*"incall"*) or on the road (*"outcall"*). In many cases, the meeting is not just sexual, but also includes time for socializing and communicating (*social time*). The meeting may also be preceded or ended by an outing to a restaurant or bar...

VIP escort: VIP (Very Important Person) refers to escorts with a certain "standing". This standing mainly emphasizes the escort's physical characteristics - whose measurements must match those of models - and, to a lesser extent, her intellectual skills. These people often work for agencies (they are therefore "professionals") and offer relatively high rates (500 to 1,000 euros an hour compared with 150 to 200 euros for a "classic" escort). VIP escorts, like courtesans, belong to the "luxury prostitution" category.

EV (one) = *"Lived Experience"*: Evaluation of a prostitute's performance by a client who has met him or her. This subjective evaluation is based on the quality of the service: duration of the act, sexual practices performed and refused, enthusiasm of the escort, physical appearance, intellectual qualities, etc. These EVs can be posted online on the escort's advert or personal website, or on specially designed sites (such as discussion forums). This is a way for customers to exchange "good plans" and prevent "scams" (or "false plans"). The tone of discourse is free and the content random. Some participants emphasize the general atmosphere of the meeting, the "professionalism" of the escort... (see EV nº 1), while others express themselves more on the technical nature of the service, using a cruder vocabulary (see EV nº 2).

EV n° 1 :

<table>
<tr><td>

Junior
Joined: August 19,
2002
Messages: 98
Location: Paris

</td><td>

Posted on 15.06.2006 5:30 am Post subject:

Heather does very little dating.
She is a very courteous, friendly and talkative young lady.
She even found me "shy" which is quite the first time.
Her physique is pleasant.
I was in a hurry and not very diligent, but she was cuddly as if I were the best of lovers.
She has a real talent for organizing a "turnkey" date. You give her a date and a place, a few hours later she gives you a choice of several hotels, takes care of the reservations etc. like a travel agency.

voilà...

</td></tr>
</table>

EV n° 2 :

<table>
<tr><td>

MCyoda
Senior

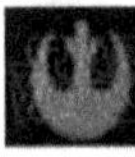

Joined: August 24, 2004
Messages: 322
Location: Planete
DAGOBA

</td><td>

Posted on 22.03.2005 1:08 am Post subject:

I fucked him, it was a month ago, rue Vaugirard, Paris 15th.

Not great, except for the natural fellatio, which is better than pompous Sandy... because she's good and her lips are nice and warm and wet...

To be tested just for the blowjob.

200 euros for the whole package!

</td></tr>
</table>

GFE (to be) = "Girl-friend experience": Used to describe the behavior of an escort who would be very natural during the service, with whom the sexual relationship is comparable to that of an official girlfriend.

Plan (un): Escort coordinates; "a good plan".

Performance (one): A venal rendezvous; sexual act.

Pross * : Prostitution

On-tour prostitute: A prostitute/escort who works for a pimp. The pimp installs her for a period - more or less short -

in a hotel in a major Western city, where she receives a large number of clients every day (often more than 10 per day), and then moves her to another city. Recruitment networks (mostly in Eastern Europe) and solicitation are carried out via the Web. The term *on tour* indicates that the prostitute is "on tour", making the "rounds" of major Western cities.

Punter (un): A rather negative term for a regular (or even very regular) customer of prostitutes, whose main aim is to "rate"/evaluate (on *EV* sites in particular) the prostitute's performance.

RV (un) = un RDV : A venal appointment.

Social time: In the prostitutional relationship, *social time* corresponds to the moment(s) other than the one(s) during which the actual sexual act takes place. It therefore refers to the various times of verbal exchange between the client and the prostitute, during the venal rendezvous as well as before or after it, during a dinner in a restaurant, for example. *Social time* helps to give a "natural" character to the paid encounter.

Taboo: A sexual practice that the escort refuses to engage in as part of a commercial relationship. In contrast, the term **"taboo-free"** refers to an escort who accepts all kinds of practices.

APPENDIX 3:

JARGON USED ON ONLINE DISCUSSION FORUMS

→ Vocabulary specific to forums in general and the Forum in particular

NB: Terms followed by an * are those used exclusively on the **Forum.**

- **Alumni *(The)**: *Forumers* who have been registered on the Forum for more than a year, and who participate regularly.
- **Avatar (an)**: Image used to designate the appearance of an Internet user in a virtual universe, such as a discussion forum. Chosen by the user himself, the avatar that represents him appears each time he logs on to a virtual universe or writes a message in a forum, so that he can be visually identified.
- **Ban**: "Eliminate"/delete a pseudonym whose messages don't respect the forum's *charter* (only the *moderators* have the means to ban a forumer).
- **Being "out of charter"**: Not respecting one or more of the rules set out in the forum's user *charter.*
- **Blog**: *Web site* consisting of a collection of posts arranged in chronological order. Each post (also called a note or article) is, like a diary or journal, an addition to the blog. The *blogger* (the person who keeps the blog) posts a text, often enriched with *hyperlinks* and multimedia elements, which readers can generally comment on.
- **Chat (un)**: Instant Internet chat room - *Chatter*: to chat on this space.
- **Charter (one):** Forum rules.

- **Edit**: Modify a *post* after publication on the forum.
- **Fake (one)**: A false story and/or a liar. This term is used to describe and denounce a rumor, a more or less crude photographic montage, or an invented story.
- **Flood**: A joke, a hijacking of a topic or typing characters, words... repeatedly, in forums or chats so that nothing is seen or understood, the forum/chat is flooded. *(see Flooder)*
- **Flooder** : To joke. Can also be used to refer to verbal overload on a forum, or mailing lists on the Internet. By extension, to **flood is** to flood a forum with messages, not necessarily to "flood" it, but simply to participate in it.
- **Flooder** (a): A person who repeatedly writes mostly useless messages on a list or forum.
- **Forumer** : A person who participates (by writing) in discussions posted online on a forum.
- **JAD = Just a dream***: (Real) meeting between Forum participants.
- **Make a cam:** Chat via instant messaging with a web cam.
- **Make an msn:** Chat via instant messaging.
- **Make an up:** Bring up a topic/discussion in a forum.
- **Moderator:** A regular user of a forum, whose role is to stimulate and stimulate exchanges between participants. He/she also assists the *moderators* in their task of ensuring compliance with forum rules. In the event of a dispute, the moderator must intervene to rectify the situation.
- **Moderator (one):** The moderator is responsible for ensuring that the rules set out in a forum's *charter are* respected, and for limiting any tensions between participants. He or she can delete *"out-of-charter"* messages, close a *thread* or *ban* a *pseudonym*.

- **MSN**: Instant messaging.
- **Multi-pseudo (a):** Forumer with several pseudonyms to his credit. Often, each pseudonym corresponds to a singular personality, and "multi-pseudos" sometimes use it to fool other participants.
- **Padlock a thread**: Close a discussion on a forum (often for reasons of non-compliance with the rules set out in the *charter*).
- **PM (one)** = *"Personal Message"*: Message sent by one forumer to another (in his personal mailbox) via the forum, but without anyone else being able to read it.
- **Post**: Write/edit a message and put it online on a forum.
- **Post**: Message from a forumer.
- **Pseudonym** : Name used on a forum and chosen by the user.
- **Smiley** = **emoticon**: Pictograms commonly used on the Internet to express emotions and feelings. These symbols, most often depicting a stylized face, consist of a series of characters to be read with the head tilted to the left. There are hundreds of them in widespread use. **Smileys** are mainly used to indicate humor, but also moments of sadness, emotions, or to express a physical attitude (sulky, mute…). **Smileys** can be found just about everywhere, mainly in *e-mail* and *newsgroup* messages. *(See the most frequently used smileys on the Forum).*
- **Topic**: General topic of an online discussion on an Internet forum.
- **Troll**: Disturber. Refers to a person, or a group of people, participating in a discussion space (such as a forum), who seeks to insidiously hijack the subject of a discussion in order to generate conflict by inciting controversy and provoking other participants. By *metonymy,* we use the term **"troll"** to describe

a message that is likely to generate controversy or that is excessively provocative, without seeking to be constructive, or that we don't want to respond to and that we are trying to discredit by naming it as such.
- **Thread:** Discussion thread.
- **Webmaster**: Website creator and manager.

→ Most frequently used abbreviations on the Forum

- **Lol** : " je rigole "
- **Mdr:** " Mort-e de rire " (Dying of laughter)
- **Modo**: "moderator
- **Pseudo** : "pseudonym

→ Smileys most used on the Forum

= I'm happy, that makes me happy		= I love
= Just kidding.		= I'm suspicious
= Hello or goodbye		= I do not understand
= I'm offended - I don't agree		= I'm overworked, tired
= Wink		= I agree - respect
= I'm skeptical		= I don't feel like explaining myself
= I'm sad		= It's forbidden - don't agree
= I am angry, upset		= I'm very happy!
= I can't believe my eyes!		I'm in great shape
= It's really funny		= I don't care

Table of Contents

Table of contents

Best sellers Max Milo Editions

Hitler's banker, Jean-François Bouchard

Confessions of a forger, Éric Piedoie Le Tiec

The Koran and the flesh, Ludovic-Mohamed Zahed

Governing by fake news, Jacques Baud

Governing by chaos, Collectif

A political history of food, Paul Ariès

Mad in U.S.A.: The ravages of the "American model",
Michel Desmurget

Mondial soccer club geopolitics, Kévin Veyssière

Putin: Game master?, Jacques Braud

Treatise on the three impostors: Moses, Jesus, Muhammad,
The Spirit of Spinoza

TV Lobotomy, Michel Desmurget